John Hamilton Adams, Granville Sharp

The Law of Retribution

A Serious Warning to Great Britain and Her Colonies

John Hamilton Adams, Granville Sharp

The Law of Retribution
A Serious Warning to Great Britain and Her Colonies

ISBN/EAN: 9783744670739

Printed in Europe, USA, Canada, Australia, Japan

Cover: Foto ©ninafisch / pixelio.de

More available books at **www.hansebooks.com**

THE LAW OF RETRIBUTION.

THE LAW OF RETRIBUTION;

OR,

A SERIOUS WARNING

TO

GREAT BRITAIN AND HER COLONIES,

Founded on unquestionable EXAMPLES of

GOD's TEMPORAL VENGEANCE

AGAINST

Tyrants, Slave-holders, and Oppressors.

The Examples are selected from *Predictions* in the Old Testament, of NATIONAL JUDGEMENTS, which (being compared with their actual Accomplishment) demonstrate "*the sure Word of Prophecy,*" as well as the *immediate Interposition of* DIVINE PROVIDENCE, *to recompence impenitent* NATIONS *according to their Works.*

By GRANVILLE SHARP.

" The People of the Land have used *Oppression*, and exercised *Robbery*, and have *vexed the Poor and Needy:* yea, they have OPPRESSED THE STRANGER WRONGFULLY," &c. " Therefore have I poured out mine Indignation upon them," &c. " Their own WAY have I recompensed upon their Heads, saith the Lord God."   Ezek. xxii. 29—31.

LONDON:

Printed by W. RICHARDSON,

For B. WHITE, at Horace's Head, in Fleet Street; and E. and C. DILLY, in the Poultry.

MDCCLXXVI.

"If thou seest the Oppression of the Poor, and violent
"perverting of Judgement and Justice in a Province,
"marvel not at the matter (*or will*) FOR HE THAT
"IS HIGHER THAN THE HIGHEST REGARDETH,"
&c. Eccles. v. 8.—"*The* Lord SAW (it) and it dis-
"pleased him that there was NO JUDGEMENT, and
"he SAW that *there was* NO MAN, and wondered
"that (*there was*) NO INTERCESSOR:" &c.—"And
"he put on the Garments of VENGEANCE for cloth-
"ing, and was clad with zeal as a cloke. ACCORD-
"ING TO THEIR DEEDS, ACCORDINGLY HE WILL
"REPAY, fury to his Adversaries, RECOMPENCE (or
"*Retribution*) TO HIS ENEMIES, TO THE ISLANDS
"HE WILL REPAY RECOMPENCE," &c. Isa. lix.—
"How long will ye judge unjustly, and accept the
"Persons of the Wicked? Defend the Poor and
"Fatherless: do Justice to the Afflicted and Needy.
"DELIVER THE POOR AND NEEDY: RID THEM
"OUT OF THE HAND OF THE WICKED." Ps. lxxxii.
2—4.—"Remove Violence and Spoil, and execute
"Judgement and Justice, TAKE AWAY YOUR EX-
"ACTIONS FROM MY PEOPLE, SAITH THE LORD
"GOD!" Ezek. xlv. 9.

THE LAW OF RETRIBUTION.

THE AFRICAN SLAVE-TRADE has been publicly supported and encouraged by *the Legislature of this Kingdom* for near a century last past; so that the *monstrous destruction of the Human Species*, which is *annually* occasioned thereby, may certainly be esteemed a *National Crime* of the most aggravating kind, which (according to the usual course of God's Providence in the World) will probably draw down some exemplary vengeance upon the unrepenting Inhabitants of this Island! And, with respect to the *British Colonies*, the

A uncha-

uncharitable practice of *Slave-holding*, especially in the West-India Islands and the more Southern Colonies, is grown up into a more enormous and destructive *Oppression* (whether we view the prodigious multitudes of the *Oppressed*, or the unconscionable severity of the *Oppressors*) than perhaps ever disgraced any other Nation at any one period of time!

The several attempts that have lately been made to justify these two branches of abominable National Iniquity by the Holy Scriptures, and especially by the permission therein granted to *the Israelites* to *purchase* and *retain Slaves* among them, have induced me to collect, from the History of *the Jews* in the several Books of Holy Scripture, some plain examples of God's Vengeance upon that particular Nation, expressly for this kind of *Oppression*; which, I hope, will sufficiently prove that *Slavery* was ever detestable in the fight of God, and confequently that a fpeedy Reformation is abfolutely neceffary (as well with refpect to the *African Slave-trade*, encouraged in this Kingdom, as the *Toleration of Slavery* in the Britifh American Dominions) if we mean to entertain the leaft hope of efcaping a fevere *National Retribution*, which (if we may judge by our prefent Civil Diffentions and horrid *mutual* Slaughters of *National Brethren*) feem ready to burft upon us!

I am well aware, indeed, how very unfafhionable it is, now-a-days, to quote *Scripture*, when matters of *Law*, *Politics*, or *Trade* are called in queftion; yet I flatter myfelf that the following examples, drawn from thence, are perfectly fuitable to my prefent point, and confequently muft have weight to convince all perfons, who fincerely acknowledge the *Truth of the Scriptures*, that we have the greateft

A 2   reafon

reason, to apprehend the infliction of some heavy Judgement from Almighty God upon these Kingdoms, on account of the monstrous load of Guilt which the British Subjects, *on each side of the Atlantic*, have incurred by the *Oppressions* above-mentioned.

In some former Tracts I have already shewn that the Servitude which the Jews, by the Mosaic-Law, were permitted to exact of *their Brethren* (even when the latter were *sold* to them) was very much *limited*; that they were not to be treated as *Bond Servants* (1), but as *Hired Servants*; that the *Servitude* could not lawfully be extended beyond *seven years* (2),

(1) "If thy *Brother* (that dwelleth) by thee be waxen "poor, and be *sold unto thee*, thou shalt not compel "him to serve as *a Bond Servant:* but as an Hired "Servant, and as a Sojourner, he shall be with thee," &c. Levit. xxv. 39, 40.

(2) "If thou buy an Hebrew Servant, six years he "shall serve, and in the seventh he shall go out free "for nothing." Exod. xxi. 2.

unless

[5]

unless the Servant loved *his Master* and Condition, and voluntarily demanded (3) of him to be continued in his Service; and that, in every other case, it was

(3) "And if the Servant shall *plainly* say, *I love* my Master, my Wife, and my Children; *I will not go out free:*" &c. Exod. xxi. 5. Thus it is evident that the Jews could not acquire *any right* to the perpetual Service of their *Brethren*, John or Thomas, except by virtue of *a voluntary Contract*, which is something similar to that Clause in the Habeas Corpus Act concerning a Contract, which I thought myself obliged to acknowledge in my former Tract as an exception to the idea of Universal *Freedom* in this Kingdom. But in neither case can the *Contract* for Service be *implied*; for in the latter the Contract must be *in writing*, and the signing be clearly proved to be *a voluntary act*, without the least suspicion of *Duress*; and in the former case it was necessary that the Servant should acknowledge, in *a Court of Record*, that he was *willing* to enter into such a Contract; for the Hebrew *Servant* could not be made a *Slave*, unless he would "*plainly say*, I love my Master," &c. "I WILL NOT GO OUT FREE: Then" (says the Text) "his Master shall bring him *unto the* JUDGES" (which answers to the public *Acknowledgement* necessary in the other case to be made in *a Court of Record)* for without this the Hebrew Master had no authority to bore the Servant's Ear in token of Bondage. Exod. xxi. 5, 6.

absolutely

abſolutely unlawful to hold a Brother Hebrew in Slavery.

I have likewiſe ſhewn, that, under the glorious Diſpenſation of the Goſpel, we are abſolutely bound to conſider ourſelves as *Citizens of the World*; that every Man whatever, without any *partial diſtinction* of Nation, Diſtance, or Complexion, muſt neceſſarily be eſteemed *our Neighbour*, and *our Brother*; and that we are abſolutely bound in Chriſtian Duty to entertain *a Diſpoſition* towards *all Mankind* as charitable and benevolent, *at leaſt*, as that which was required of the Jews, under the Law, towards their *national Brethren*; and, conſequently, that it is abſolutely unlawful for thoſe, *who call themſelves Chriſtians*, to exact of *their Brethren* (I mean *their Brethren of the Univerſe*) a more burthenſome Service than that to which the Jews were limited with reſpect to their
Brethren.

Brethren of the House of Israel; and the Slavery, or involuntary Bondage, of *a Brother Israelite* was absolutely forbid.

These premises naturally lead us to consider the severe NATIONAL JUDGEMENTS which the Jews brought upon themselves principally *by exceeding these very limitations* which I have here specified: and the inevitable conclusion to be drawn from these examples is, that we are *absolutely* in danger of THE LIKE JUDGEMENTS, if we do not immediately put a stop to all *similar Oppression* by *National Authority*: because an uncharitable extension of the *said limits*, by those who call themselves Christians, will certainly be, at least, *as heinous in the sight of God* as the OPPRESSION OF BRETHREN under the Law; and probably much more so, if we consider the purity and benevolence which is required of all Men under the Gospel Dispensation: and I have clearly

clearly proved (I trust) that the permission to the Israelites, to keep *Bondmen of the Heathen* (or more properly the *Nations*, הגוים) *that were round about them*, and of "*the* Children of *the Strangers* "*that dwelt among them*," cannot be extended to *any other People* whatever except *the Israelites* themselves; and that even to them it was only *temporary*, during the Dispensation of the Mosaic Law, whilst they possessed the Land of Canaan, the former Inhabitants of which (*viz*. the seven abominable *Nations* of Palestine, expresly mentioned by name in the seventh Chapter of Deuteronomy, where the same Heb. Noun גוים, rendered *Heathen* in the former Text, is properly expressed by the English word *Nations*) the Israelites were expresly directed to drive out, kill, and destroy, *without pity* (4), and to make *no Covenant*

(4) " Thine eye shall have *no pity* upon them." Deut. vii. 16.

with

with them (5) : and I hope I have also proved that *the remainder* of these particular wicked Nations, thus expressly doomed to destruction, were undoubtedly " the *Heathen*" (or *Nations*) " *that dwelt* " *round about*" the Israelites, and " *the* " *Children of the Strangers,*" whom (and *whom alone*) it was lawful to hold *in perpetual Bondage*; for otherwise that permission cannot be reconciled to God's positive Commands, given in the same Law, to *love* the *Stranger*. " The Lord " your God is God of Gods, and Lord " of Lords, a great God, a mighty and a " terrible, *which regardeth not Persons*" (so that this was apparently a general Law, or Rule of Conduct, towards *all Persons*, except the People of those *particular Nations* which were expressly, *by name*, condemned to destruction by the hands of the Israelites, in other parts of

(5) " Thou shalt make *no Covenant* with them, " nor *shew Mercy* unto them," &c. Deut. vii. 2.

B the

the Law, for their abominable wickedness) "nor taketh Reward: he doth ex-
"ecute the Judgement of the Father-
"less and Widow, and *loveth the Stran-*
"*ger*, in giving him food and raiment.
"LOVE YE THEREFORE *the*
"*Stranger*" (and the Almighty inculcates a sympathetic concern for the welfare and happiness of *Strangers*, by reminding the Israelites of their own unhappy situation formerly in a *strange* country) "for ye" (says the Text) "were
"*Strangers* in the Land of Egypt."
Deut. x. 17 to 19. See also Levit. xix. 33, 34. "*Thou shalt love him*" (that is, *the Stranger*) "*as thyself*; for ye were
"*Strangers* in the Land of Egypt."

National Wickedness, from the beginning of the World, has generally been visited with *National* Punishments: and surely no *National* Wickedness can be more heinous in the sight of God, than

than a public toleration of *Slavery and Oppression!* for Tyranny (in whatsoever shape it appears) must necessarily be esteemed a presumptuous breach of that Divine Command, in which " *all Law is fulfilled*" (Gal. v. 14.) *viz.* " Thou " shalt love thy Neighbour as thyself." Levit. xix. 18.

The Histories of all Nations, indeed, afford tremendous examples of *God's Vengeance* against Tyrants; but no History is so proper to illustrate this subject (which now so nearly concerns us) as that of the Jews : for as the Knowledge of the *Divine Law* was revealed in a more particular manner to *that People,* and to others *only through them,* so the effect even of their Disobedience was an exemplary demonstration, from time to time, of *God's Vengeance,* as well as of *his Mercy,* for the instruction of all other Nations, amongst whom they are now difperfed, as living monuments of the fame to this very day: and we have the authority of an Apoftle (6) to affert, that " all thefe things happened " unto them for enfamples; and they " are written" (fays he) " for our ad- " monition, upon whom the ends of " the world are come."

One of the firft and moft signal inftances of Mercy which the Almighty was pleafed to fhew that People, after they *became a Nation*, was, the reftoring them to their *Natural Freedom* from the deplorable *Slavery* in which they were detained by a tyrannical Egyptian Monarch (7): and the tremendous

Judge-

---

(6) 1 Cor. x. 11.

(7) —" the Children of Ifrael fighed by reafon of " *the Bondage*, and *they cried*; and their cry came " up unto God *by reafon of the Bondage*: and God " *heard their groaning*," &c. Exod. ii. 23, 24.

" And

Judgements whereby this deliverance was effected (*viz.* the Plagues of Egypt) are so many signal examples of *God's severe Vengeance against Slave-holders*, which ought to be had in everlasting remembrance, to warn all Nations of the World against the unnatural and baneful practice of *keeping Slaves*.

This deliverance from *Bondage* was frequently mentioned, even in the words of God himself, by his Prophets, from time to time (as I have before remarked) —" Thus saith the Lord" *(i. e.* Jehovah) " God of Israel: I brought you up
" from Egypt, and brought you forth
" *out of the House of Bondage* ;" (מבית עבדים, more *literally* " from the House

---

" And the Lord said, I have *surely seen the Affliction*
" *of my People* which are in Egypt, and have *heard*
" *their cry* by reason of their *Task-masters:* for I
" know their Sorrows, and I am come down *to deli-*
" *ver them* out of the hand of the Egyptians."
Exod. iii. 7, 8.

" *of*

"*of Slaves*") " and *I delivered you* out
" of the hand of the Egyptians, and
" out of the hand of *all that oppressed*
" *you*," &c. Judges vi. 8. —— " I re-
" moved his *Shoulder from the Burden*;
" his *Hands were delivered from the*
" *Pots* (8) : thou calledst in trouble,
" and I delivered thee." Psal. lxxxi.
6, 7.

The Israelites themselves were also particularly directed *to remember* this signal exertion of Divine Mercy and Power in the cause of *Popular Freedom:* " *Remember* that thou wast *a Servant* " *(viz. a Slave)* " in the Land of Egypt, " and that the Lord thy God *brought* " *thee out* thence *through a mighty hand,* " and by a stretched-out arm," &c. Deut. v. 15.

(8) In like manner there are multitudes of poor people retained in *a deplorable Bondage*, even to this day, in *the Potteries* of China.

It

It was surely for the moral purpose of stirring up in the Israelites a sympathetic concern for the Sufferings of the *Oppressed*, and more particularly of *Oppressed Strangers*, that they were so frequently reminded of their own former deplorable condition *in Slavery*, and of their miraculous *Deliverance* from thence; being expressly referred to their *own Feelings* and *Remembrance* of the cruel *foreign* Tyranny, which they themselves had so lately experienced in Egypt: — " thou shalt not oppress *a Stranger* : " for *ye* KNOW THE HEART " (נפש, properly THE SOUL) " OF A " STRANGER, seeing ye were *Strangers* in the Land of Egypt." Exod. xxiii. 9.

God also gave the Israelites due warning of the Danger of *Oppression*, by declaring that he would SURELY revenge the Cause of the injured *Stranger* :
" Thou

" Thou shalt neither *vex a Stranger*,
" nor *oppress him*; for ye were *Strangers*
" in the Land of Egypt. Ye shall not
" afflict any Widow or fatherless Child.
" If thou afflict them in any wise, and
" *they cry at all unto me, I will* SURELY
" *hear their cry*" (mark this, ye African
Traders *of this Island*, and ye *West-India*
and *British American* Slave-holders! for
ye are all guilty of the like abominable
Oppressions, and God will SURELY
avenge the Cause of *the Oppressed)* " and
" my wrath shall wax hot, and I will
" kill you with the sword, and your
" Wives shall be Widows, and your
" Children fatherless." Exod. xxii. 21
to 24.

And have not the careless Inhabitants of Great Britain and her Colonies too much reason also to apprehend that *the same God* (who *professes* to *hear the cry* of oppressed *Strangers*, if they *cry at all*

all unto him) will, sooner or later, visit these Kingdoms with some signal mark of his Displeasure, for the notorious *Oppression* of an almost innumerable multitude of poor *African Strangers*, that are harrassed, and continually wearing out, with a most shameful involuntary Servitude in the *British Colonies!* nay, and that by a public Toleration, under the sanction of Laws to which the Monarchs of England, from time to time, by the advice of their Privy Counsellors, have given *the Royal Assent*, and thereby rendered themselves Parties in *the Oppression*, and (it is to be feared) Partakers of the Guilt!

Let us not forget, before it is too late, that the Almighty has not only declared himself ready to " HEAR THE CRY" *of the oppressed Stranger*, but hath deigned to add to his glorious Name, *Jehovah*, a brief *Remembrance* of his merciful inter-

position

position in behalf of an *enslaved Nation:* " I am the Lord your God" (or *Jehovah* your God, said the Almighty to the Israelites) " which *brought thee out of* " *the Land of Egypt, out of the House of* " *Bondage.*" Exod. xx. 1. Thus the Almighty Deliverer from *Slavery* vouchsafed to set his own Divine Example before the eyes of his redeemed People, to excite Benevolence and Thankfulness; and the like Remembrance of that glorious Redemption from *Slavery* was very frequently repeated from time to time; which the Scriptures sufficiently testify: but alas! the Israelites profited so little by these wholesome lessons, that it became necessary, no less frequently, to remind them of *the dreadful Vengeance* which would inevitably overtake them for their notorious *Oppressions of the Poor*; for their unjust Exactions of *involuntary and unrewarded Service*; and for exceeding the

limi-

limitations of *Bondage* (already recited) which the Law expressly enjoined!

" For the *Oppression* of the Poor, for
" the *Sighing* of the Needy, now will
" I *arise,* saith the Lord; and will set
" him in safety from him that puffeth
" at him," or " that would ensnare
" him." Psal. xii. 5.

The Princely Prophet Isaiah plainly declared to them, that their public Fasts and outward Humiliations were not only vain, but even offensive to God, while *such notorious Oppressions* continued among them. " Behold" (said he) " in the
" day of your Fast, you find Pleasure,
" and *exact all your Labours.*" (9) lviii. 3.
And

---

(9) Sunt inter quos Belgæ, qui hic intelligunt *Opera Servilia,* quæ a *Servis* & *Ancillis* hoc ipso die *rigide exigebantur,* ut aliis diebus. Ὁι ὁ—" Πανίας τȣς ὑποχειριȣς ὑμων ὑπονυσσετε," *Omnes Subjectos vobis affligitis:* quæ lectio (says Vitringa) absque emendatione facile subsistit.

And again, —" Is it such a Fast that I have chosen? a day for a Man to afflict his Soul? is it to bow down his head as a bulrush?" &c. " Is not this the Fast that I have chosen?— to loose *the Bands of Wickedness*, to undo *the heavy Burthens*" (or rather *the Bundles of the Yoke,* אגדות מוטה plainly referring to the severe and *unjust Bondage of the Poor)* " and TO LET THE OPPRESSED GO FREE, and that YE BREAK EVERY YOKE?"—" Is it not to deal thy Bread to the Hungry, and to bring the Poor that are *cast out*" (or rather to bring the Poor that are *reduced,* or *depressed*, *viz.* as it were by Tyrants; for so the word מרודים seems more properly to signify in this place) " *to thy House?*" &c. Compare this

---

istit.—And a little afterwards he adds, Prior interpretatio *de Operibus Servorum* aut *molestis exactionibus Subditorum,* magna se commendat specie, estque mihi in eam pronior animus.

with

with Deut. xxiii. 15, 16. (9) And he warned them of the Divine Justice that would pursue them for their Oppression and tyrannical Treatment of the Poor.

"The Lord standeth up to plead,
"and standeth to judge the People!
"The Lord will enter into Judge-
"ment with the Ancients (or *Senators*)
"of his People, and *the Princes* thereof:
"for ye have eaten up the Vineyard;
"*the Spoil of the Poor is in your Houses!*
"What mean ye that ye *beat my*
"*People to pieces*, and grind the Faces
"of the Poor?" saith the Lord of Hosts! Isa. iii. 13 to 15.

The wicked practices whereby the Israelites reduced their poor *Brethren* to

---

(9) *Thou shalt not deliver unto his Master the Servant which is escaped from his Master* unto thee: he shall *dwell with thee (even)* among you, in that place which he shall choose, *in one of thy gates* where it liketh him best: thou shalt not *oppress him*. Deut. xxiii. 15, 16.

Slavery

Slavery are described by the Prophet Amos: " Hear this, O ye that *swallow up the Needy*, even to make *the Poor of the Land to fail*, saying, When will the New Moon be gone, that we may sell Corn ? and the Sabbath, that we may set forth Wheat, making the Ephah small, and the Shekel great, and falsifying the Ballances by Deceit ? That *we may buy the Poor for Silver* (10) *and the Needy for a Pair of Shoes*" (that is, comparatively speaking, at a most contemptible price ! whereby we may presume that *Slave-markets* were not so notoriously established at that time as at present ; and that the *Bidders* were *few*, though the *Oppressed* were *many)* " yea, and sell the Refuse of the Wheat ? The Lord hath sworn by the Excellency of Ja-

---

(10) " Ideo ut ubi solvere non poterunt, dent se " nobis *in Servitutem*, ut mos erat illarum Gentium." *Grotius* in locum.

" cob,

" cob, *surely I will never forget any of*
" *these works. Shall not the Land tremble*
" *for this, and every one mourn that*
" *dwelleth therein?*" &c. Amos viii.
4 to 8.

Here is a solemn Appeal from God to the *Human Understanding*: " Shall not
" the Land tremble *for this!*" that is, for this same *abominable Oppression* of the Poor *(the buying them for Slaves)* in which Great Britain and her Colonies are infinitely more guilty than the People to whom this appeal was made! and " *shall not the Land*" (therefore) " *even our Land, tremble for*
" *this, and every one mourn that dwelleth*
" *therein?*" &c. Surely " God will
" never forget any of these *Works*," my Countrymen!

The Prophet Jeremiah manifestly alluded to the like deceitful practices

of the Jews (whereby they reduced the Poor to *Slavery*) when he made a solemn protest against them in the Name of God :—" Your sins" (said he) " have
" withholden good things from you.
" For among my People are found
" wicked (men): they lay wait as he
" *that setteth Snares* ; THEY SET A
" TRAP, THEY CATCH MEN. As a
" Cage (or Coup) is full of Birds, so
" are their Houses full of Deceit :
" therefore they are become great, and
" waxen rich. They are waxen fat,
" they shine : yea, they overpass the
" deeds of the Wicked; they judge
" not the cause, the cause of the Fatherless,
" yet they prosper ; and the right
" of the Needy do they not judge.
" Shall I not visit for these things ?
" saith the Lord ! Shall not *my Soul be*
" *avenged on such a Nation as this ?*" &c. Jer. v. 26 to 29. Here again the Almighty plainly appeals to the Human Under-

Understanding concerning the Propriety, or rather the Necessity, of exerting the Divine Vengeance against such an *Oppressive Nation!*

And yet how inconsiderable was the crime of the Jewish Nation in this respect, if compared with the *numerous Bondage* and with the unbounded Oppression of the poor Negroes in the British Colonies? Have we not therefore just reason to fear that God will " *visit* " *for these things?*" Does not the Word of God, which cannot change, appeal to us, my Countrymen, as well as to the Jews?—" *Shall not my Soul*" (saith the Lord!) " *be avenged on such a Nation as this?*"

The same Prophet, in the next chapter, declares *the Divine Vengeance* to be at hand:—" For thus hath the Lord " of Hosts said,—Hew ye down Trees, " and

" and caft a Mount *againft Jerufalem.*
" This (is) the City to be vifited! fhe
" is *wholly Oppreffion* in the midft of
" her. As a Fountain cafteth out her
" Waters, fo fhe cafteth out her Wick-
" ednefs: *Violence and Spoil* is heard in
" her; before me continually is *Grief*
" *and Wounds!* Be thou inftructed, O
" Jerufalem! left my Soul depart from
" thee: left I make thee defolate, a
" Land not inhabited!" Jer. vi. 6 to 8.

But in vain were the Warnings of the Prophet, till *the Judgements* themfelves began to appear *in all the horrors of a hopelefs War*, which began in the ninth year (11) of King Zedekiah's reign,

(11) " And it came to pafs in the ninth year of his
" reign, in the tenth month, in the tenth day of the
" month, that Nebuchadnezzar King of Babylon
" came, he and all his hoft, againft Jerufalem, and
" pitched againft it: and they built forts againft it
" round about." 2 Kings xxv. 1.—" In the ninth
" year

reign, notwithstanding that the Monarch had previously rendered himself secure (as he thought) by his military preparations (in sending for *Horses* and *Men* from Egypt, to complete his standing Army) and had also made Pharaoh (another presumptuous military Tyrant) his Ally, which encouraged him to break his Oath and Covenant with the King of Babylon.

But " when Nebuchadnezzar King
" of Babylon, and *all his Army, and all*
" *the Kingdoms of the Earth, of his Do-*
" *minion, and all the People, fought*
" *against Jerusalem, and against all the*
" *Cities thereof*"—then God ordered his Prophet to remind Zedekiah of that dreadful Vengeance, Defeat and Cap-

" year of Zedekiah King of Judah, in the tenth month,
" came Nebuchadnezzar King of Babylon, and all
" his army, against Jerusalem, and they besieged it,"
&c. Jer. xxxix. 1. See also chap. lii. ver. 9.

tivity,

tivity, which had so often before been denounced as the necessary consequences of *Oppression and Injustice!* — " Thus "saith the Lord, the God of Israel" (*viz.* to Jeremiah): " Go, and speak " to Zedekiah King of Judah, and tell " him, Thus saith the Lord; behold, " I will *give this City into the hand* of " the King of Babylon; and he shall " burn it with fire. And thou shalt " not escape out of his hand, but shalt " surely be taken, and delivered into " his hand; and *thine eyes shall behold* " *the eyes of the King of Babylon*, and he " shall speak with thee *mouth to mouth*, " and thou shalt go to Babylon," &c. Jer. xxxiv. 1 to 3.

The impending *Vengeance* being then become *visible*, and consequently more tremendous, by the near approach of the Babylonian Army, that irresistible instrument in the hand of God, by which

which the Jews had so often been subdued, the King's stubborn heart began to relent, and his *military confidence* to forsake him, . which had before encouraged his *Injustice* ; his firmness in *Worldly Politics* was shaken, and yielded to a sense of Guilt! It was upon this return of Conscience and right Reason that Zedekiah sent two Messengers, Passur and Zephaniah, to Jeremiah, saying, " Enquire, I pray thee, of the " Lord for us; for Nebuchadnezzar " King of Babylon maketh war against " us; if so be the Lord will *deal with* " *us* according to *all his wondrous works,* " that he may go up from us," &c. See chap. xxi. ver. 1 and 2. But a very unwelcome answer was given to the Messengers, to be returned to their Monarch; for the Prophet confirmed all the heavy Judgements (12) which had
before

(12) " Then said Jeremiah unto them, Thus shall " ye say to Zedekiah: Thus saith the Lord God of
" Israel;

before been denounced, as well against the King, expresly by name, as against the City and its iniquitous Inhabitants, whose notorious *Oppressions* were now *to be* RECOMPENSED *upon their own heads*, MEASURE FOR MEASURE: — " Now
" is the end come upon thee, and *I will*
" *send mine anger upon thee, and will judge*

" Israel; Behold, I will turn back the weapons of
" war that are in your hands, wherewith ye fight
" against the King of Babylon, and against the Chal-
" deans which besiege you without the walls; and I
" will bring them *into the midst* of this City. And I
" myself will fight against you, with an outstretched
" arm, and with a strong arm, even in anger, and in
" fury, and in great wrath. And I will smite the
" Inhabitants of this City, both Man and Beast:
" they shall die of a great Pestilence. And afterwards,
" saith the Lord, I will deliver *Zedekiah King of Ju-*
" *dah*, and *his Servants*, and *the People*, and such as
" are left in this City, from the Pestilence, from the
" Sword, and from the Famine, into the hand of
" Nebuchadnezzar King of Babylon, and into the
" hand of their Enemies, and into the hand of those
" that seek their Life; and he shall smite them with
" the Edge of the Sword; he shall not spare them,
" neither have Pity, nor have Mercy!" Jer. xxi.
5 to 7.

" *thee*

"*thee according to thy ways*, and will
"RECOMPENSE *upon thee all thine abo-*
"*minations,*" &c. Ezek. vii. 3. See also
the 4th, 8th, and 9th verses, to the same
effect. And afterwards, in the 11th
verse, one of the principal causes of
GOD's *Vengeance* is mentioned:—" *Vio-*
"*lence*" (said the Prophet) " is risen
" up into *a Rod of Wickedness:* none of
" them shall remain, nor of their mul-
" titude, nor of any of their's; neither
" shall there be wailing for them. The
" time is come, the day draweth near!"
&c.——And again, in the 23d verse:—
" *Make a Chain*" (said the Prophet);
" for the Land is full of *bloody Crimes,*
" and the City is full of *Violence.*
" Wherefore *I will bring the worst* of
" the Heathen, and they shall possess
" their houses," &c. — " Destruction
" cometh; and they shall seek peace,
" and there shall be none. Mischief
" shall come upon mischief, and rumour
                                   " shall

" shall be upon rumour," &c.—" The King shall mourn, and the Prince shall be clothed with desolation, and the Hands of the People of the Land shall be troubled: *I will do unto them after their* (own) *way, and according to their* deserts" (or rather *their own judgements*) " will I judge them; and they shall know that I am the Lord." —Again, in the 12th chapter, the same reason is clearly assigned for the pouring out of God's Vengeance:—" Say unto the People of the Land, Thus saith the Lord God of the Inhabitants of Jerusalem and of the Land of Israel; They shall eat their Bread with Carefulness; and drink their Water with Astonishment, that her Land may be desolate from all that is therein, *because of* THE VIOLENCE *of them that dwell therein.*" Ezek. xii. 19. The nature of this baneful *Violence*, which occasioned their *destruction*, is more particularly

cularly described by the same Prophet, in chap. xxii. ver. 7.—" *in the midst of* " *thee*" (still speaking of Jerusalem) " have they dealt by *Oppression* with " *the Stranger*" (mark this, ye British Slave-dealers and Slave-holders); " in " thee have they vexed the Fatherless " and the Widow. Thou hast de- " spised mine holy things, and hast pro- " faned my Sabbaths. In thee are men " that carry tales to shed Blood: and " in thee they eat upon the mountains: " in the midst of thee they commit " lewdness," &c.—" One hath com- " mitted abomination with his Neigh- " bour's Wife: and another hath " lewdly defiled his Daughter-in-law," &c.—" In thee have they taken *gifts* " *to shed Blood*: thou hast taken Usury " and Increase, and thou hast greedily " gained of thy Neighbours by Extor- " tion, and hast forgotten me, saith the " Lord God. Behold, *therefore*, I have

E " smitten

" smitten mine hand at thy dishonest
" gain which thou hast made, and at
" thy Blood which hath been in the
" midst of thee," &c. Ezek. xxii. 7, &c.

Oh that the Subjects of the British Empire would seriously compare these crimes with their own practices! they would then, surely, be sensible of their danger; and that they have reason to expect the like, or rather much heavier, Judgements, than those denounced against the Jews! For, besides the notorious *Adulteries*, and other acts of *Lewdness*, which many amongst us (from the frequency of such crimes) commit, even without shame or remorse, we have far exceeded the guilt of the Jews, I fear, in many of the other points also which provoked the Vengeance of the Almighty against them! What " *Violence*" amongst the Jews, before their Captivity, was ever
" *risen*

"*risen up into*" so destructive "*a Rod of Wickedness*" — as the AFRICAN SLAVE-TRADE, now carried on chiefly by our *Liverpool* and *Bristol* Merchants? What "*bloody crime*" among the Jews was more notorious, and more wickedly premeditated, than the late *Invasion* and *Conquest* of the poor innocent CARRIBEES at ST. VINCENT's? And what Nation hath "*dealt by Oppression with the Stranger*" so generally, so inhumanly, and in so great a degree, as our BRITISH AMERICAN SLAVE-HOLDERS!—Have we not ample reason to expect that the same tremendous decree will, in God's Justice, be fulfilled upon these Kingdoms?—"*Destruction* cometh: and they shall seek Peace, and there shall be none. Mischief shall come upon mischief, and rumour upon rumour," &c. &c. &c. —" I will do unto them after *their* (own) *way*, and according to *their* (own)

" (own) *Judgements* will I judge them!" &c.

Nevertheless, God was pleased to offer the Jews a Choice in *their Fate*,—either to forsake their wicked King (who had forfeited all right to govern, by his neglect of *Justice* and *Natural Right*) and to fall away to the King's Enemies, the Chaldeans; or else to perish miserably in the City, and partake of it's Destruction!—"And unto this People" (said God to the Prophet Jeremiah) " thou
" shalt say, Thus saith the Lord; Be-
" hold, I set before you the way of
" *Life*, and the way of *Death*. He that
" abideth in this City shall die by the
" Sword, and by the Famine, and by
" the Pestilence: but he *that goeth*
" *out, and falleth to the Chaldeans that*
" *besiege you, he shall live, and his Life*
" *shall be unto him for a Prey*," &c. Jer. xxi. 8, 9.

The

The Prophet, however, was directed to add to his message a word of advice to the *King* and *Court*, which shews that a seasonable repentance might, even then, have saved the State, and turned away the impending *Vengeance*.

It was such advice, too, as every other Monarch, who tolerates any *unnatural Bondage* or *Oppression* in his Dominions, ought seriously to consider, because the event proved it to be the best means of averting God's Anger, if the King had but persevered in it.—" And touching
" *the House of the King of Judah*" (continued the Prophet) " say,—Hear ye
" the Word of the Lord, O House of
" David—thus saith the Lord; *Exe-*
" *cute Judgement* in the morning, and
" *deliver him that is spoiled* out of the
" hand of the *Oppressor*, lest my Fury
" go out like Fire, and burn that none
" can quench *(it)*, because of the evil
" of

" of your doings." Jer. xxi. 12. This is a manifest declaration that *the Neglect of* JUSTICE *and* RIGHT, *and the Toleration of* OPPRESSION, were the principal causes of God's heavy Vengeance against *that Royal House!*

The same advice was, by God's Command, repeated by the Prophet to *the King himself* IN HIS PALACE (see the next chapter):—" Thus saith the Lord;
" Go down to THE HOUSE of the King
" of Judah, *and speak* THERE *this word*,
" and say, Hear the word of the Lord,
" *O King of Judah*, that sittest *upon the*
" *Throne of David*, thou, and thy Ser-
" vants, and thy People that enter in by
" these Gates" (that is, all Persons what-
" ever that *enter in by*" *the Palace-gates*, plainly including *the whole Court*, before whom the Prophet was to deliver his message): " Thus saith the Lord;
" *Execute* ye JUDGEMENT and RIGH-
" TEOUSNESS,

" TEOUSNESS, and *deliver the Spoiled*
" *out of the hand of* THE OPPRES-
" SOR; and do no wrong, DO NO
" VIOLENCE TO THE STRAN-
" GER (13)," &c. — " For if ye do
" this thing indeed" (that is, if ye will
execute Judgement and Righteousness, deli-
ver the Oppressed, &c.) " then shall there
" enter in *by the Gates of this House*
" Kings sitting upon the Throne of
" David" (or rather " that sit," *i. e.*
reign, " for David upon his Throne")
" riding in Chariots and on Horses, he
" and his Servants, and his People"
(that is, the Court should continue and
prosper). " But if ye will not hear
" THESE WORDS, *I swear by my-*
" *self, saith the Lord*" (*i. e.* Jehovah)

(13) And what " *Wrong*" or " *Violence to the Stran-*
" *ger*" can be more *oppressive* than that of detaining
him in an *involuntary Servitude*, WITHOUT WAGES,
in a miserable, wretched *Bondage*, worse than that of
brute Beasts!

2 " that

"that THIS HOUSE" *(i. e.* the Palace) "shall become a desolation." Jer. xxii. 1 to 5. So that *the whole Court* were as much interested to promote a speedy Reformation, as *the King himself.* Thus it is plain that *the King and Court* had also a Choice given them of *Life* and *Death,* as well as the People; and, consequently, that the Judgements denounced were only *conditional,* in case the warning was neglected; for it is manifest that God mercifully tendered to them *(even at the eve of their destruction)* a continuance of the Monarchy (viz. "*Kings sitting upon the Throne of* "*David*") if they would but resolve to "*execute* JUDGEMENT *and* RIGHTE-"OUSNESS;" to "*deliver the Spoiled* "*out of the hand of the* OPPRESSOR;" and to "*do no Wrong,* NO VIOLENCE, "*to* THE STRANGER," &c. But the Prophet also added much more *advice* to *the King and his Court,* though he was

nor

not "*made of the King's Council* (14);" for he boldly warned the Monarch by the tremendous examples of God's Judgements upon three of his immediate Predeceſſors in the Kingdom; two of whom were *his own Brothers*, the Sons

(14) When a ſimilar warning was given by a former Prophet to a wicked and inconſiderate Predeceſſor of *Zedekiah*, concerning *God's impending Vengeance* for his miſconduct, the haughty Monarch, puffed up with vain notions of his Royal Importance, arrogantly impoſed ſilence on the Prophet, becauſe he had undertaken the office of *an Adviſer* or *Counſellor* to the King without *the etiquette* or formality of a Court Appointment:—" *Art thou made of the King's Council?*" (ſaid the Monarch:) " forbear; why ſhouldeſt thou *be ſmitten?*"—Upon which the Prophet *forbore* indeed *to reaſon with him*; but immediately pronounced upon him the ſevere ſentence of God's Condemnation, ſaying, " I know that God hath determined to deſtroy " thee, becauſe thou haſt done this, and haſt not " hearkened unto *my Counſel:*" and it is remarkable, that, after *rejecting the Counſel* of God, the *very next Counſel* which this imperious Monarch was pleaſed to adopt was attended with the moſt dangerous and humiliating conſequences, *both to King and Kingdom,* that could poſſibly have happened! nothing leſs than the delivery of both into the abſolute power of their

F   Enemies!

Sons of King Jofiah; and the third *his own Nephew*, whom he immediately fucceeded. They were all particularly mentioned by him in the proper order of their refpective reigns, as we find by the copy of his Meffage or Remonftrance, preferved in the Collection of his Prophecies; and, throughout the faid Remonftrance, frequent allufions are made to the principal caufes of the failure and deftruction of each of them, which afford a moft ftriking and interefting Leffon to Kings and Governors *in general*; but it muft have been *more particularly* affecting to Zedekiah, if we confider his critical fituation at the

Enemies! for after he had *filenced* the Prophet, " then" (fays the Text) " Amaziah King of Judah TOOK " ADVICE, and fent to Joafh, the Son of Jehoahaz, " the Son of Jehu, King of Ifrael, faying, Come, " let us fee one another in the face."——The war was *unjuft* and *unreafonable*; and, providentially, the King and his *wicked Advifers* were punifhed by the effects of their own *unprincipled Counfel*. See 2 Chron. xxv. 16——24.

time

time the Message was delivered to him, and that the Examples of *Vengeance*, to which the Prophet referred him, were *actually accomplished* in the Persons of his *nearest Relations* and *Predecessors*, who were successively *deprived of their Royal Dignity*, and carried away IN CHAINS into a *slavish Captivity*; the very fate which, the Prophet assured him, was to be his own!

But before I recite the remainder of God's Message to *the Court of Zedekiah*, it will be necessary for me to give some general account of that Monarch and of his immediate Predecessors, in order that the Remonstrance, in which they are all distinctly mentioned, may be more easily understood by the generality of Readers. It will likewise be necessary for me to prove, that the whole 22d Chapter of Jeremiah is included in that *Message*, or *Remonstrance*, which the Prophet was then to deliver in the presence of the *whole Court* of Zedekiah. And I propose to insert also some remarks, as they occur, concerning the Prophet himself, and the order of time, in which he delivered the several tremendous predictions of GOD's *Vengeance* against these wicked Princes.

Zedekiah was the Son of that excellent Prince Josiah King of Judah, on whose account, expressly, *the dreadful Vengeance*, due to that wicked Nation, was postponed for several years, *viz.* till after his death.

The Scriptures mention four Sons of King Josiah, *viz.* " the first-born, Jo-
" hanan (or John); the second, Je-
" hoiakim; the third, Zedekiah; and
" the fourth, Shallum." 1 Chron. iii. 15.—What became of the eldest Son
Johanan,

Johanan, or John, is not recorded (15), but all the others afcended the Throne of David; and firſt of all, the youngeſt Son *Shallum*, whom, on the death of King Joſiah, " *the People of the Land* " *took*, and" (as it ſeems, without re-

(15) ——" this *Johanan*" (ſays Biſhop Patrick) " is " thought by many to be the ſame with *Jehoahaz*, " who ſucceeded *Joſiah* in the Throne. But he" (meaning *Jehoahaz)* " was not his firſt-born, being but " twenty-three years old when the People made him " King; and after three months time his Brother, " being put in his place, is ſaid to be twenty-five " years old. 2 Kings xxiii. 31, 36. Petavius" (continues the Biſhop). " hath ſaid a great deal about " this, in his Annotations upon Epiphanius ad " Hæreſ. Epicur. p. 18. But after all" (ſays the learned Biſhop) " *I take the truth to be, that* JOHANAN " WAS HIS ELDEST SON, *but died before his Father:* " and therefore is not mentioned in the Book of " Kings; as" (continues he) " *Jehoahaz* is not men- " tioned here, being made King by the People of the " Land, and preſently dethroned."—In the latter part of this remark, however, the worthy Biſhop is apparently miſtaken; for the ſame King, who was ſometimes called *Jehoahaz*, is certainly *mentioned* in that very Text (1 Chron. iii. 15.) on which the Biſhop made this remark, though mentioned, indeed, under a different name, *viz. Shallum*.

him *at Jerusalem* (18) (2 Chron. xxxvi. 3.) and afterwards "PUT HIM IN BANDS "at *Riblah* (19) in the Land of *Hamath*, "that

(18) " And the King of Egypt *put him down at* " *Jerusalem*, and condemned the Land in an hundred " talents of silver, and a talent of gold." 2 Chron. xxxvi. 3.

(19) RIBLAH was the fatal place where King *Zedekiah* was afterwards *judged* and *condemned* by the King of Babylon, and where *his Sons were slain before his eyes*. Jer. lii. 9. The Text also informs us, that " he" (the King of Babylon) "*slew also all the Princes* " *of Judah in* RIBLAH." Jer. lii. 10. There is something very remarkable in the meaning of these names, *Riblah* and *Hamath*, when compared with the *dreadful Vengeance* executed therein. *Riblah* (רבלה) was capable of being interpreted (though it likewise has a different meaning) as follows, *viz.* " Rixa"—" aut " *jurgium* inveteratum vel conturbatum, five *jurgium* " defluens;" (fee the Interpretation of Scripture Names annexed to the London Polyglot, Vol. VI.) and HAMATH (חמת) " *Ira* vel *indignatio*, aut *calor*," *&c. (ibid.)*; that is, the City of *Strife*, or *severe Chiding*, in the Land of *Wrath*, or *fiery Indignation*. Now it must appear very remarkable, I say, if we consider the interpretation of which these names are capable, that God should incline two foreign Conquerors (who had no connection with each other, but, on the

contrary,

" that he might not reign in *Jerufalem*" (2 Kings xxiii. 33) (20) there being, probably, fome reafon to apprehend, that he would attempt to fupplant his elder brother *Eliakim*, whom the Egyptian Conqueror had thought proper to fet up in his ftead upon " *the Throne of Da-*
" *vid*;" and therefore, to fecure the

contrary, were mortal Enemies) to execute his *Vengeance* upon different Kings of Judah *exactly at the fame place*, *viz.* the City of *Strife*, in the Land of *Wrath :* infomuch that one would fuppofe thefe names to be given afterwards, in remembrance of God's *fevere Vengeance* already executed therein ! And yet, we find, they were the ancient names of thofe places, mentioned in Mofes' account of the Ifraelitifh boundary, Numb. xxxiv. 8, 11. And though the names are really capable of bearing a different and more favourable interpretation, yet, to the Jews, who were nice obfervers concerning the real meaning of names, the poffibility of interpreting the names of thefe fatal places, in the awful fenfe which I have mentioned, muft render the accomplifhment of *God's Vengeance* therein much more ftriking and remarkable !

(20) " And Pharaoh-Nechoh *put him in bands* at " Riblah in the Land of Hamath, *that he might not* " *reign in Jerufalem*," &c. 2 Kings xxiii. 33.

sue exactly *the same method* in restoring " *the Sceptre of Judah*" to " *the House of David*," and in declaring the Establishment of *the National Law* and *Religion*, by putting a respectful memorial of the sacred Name of *Jehovah* upon the new-raised Monarchs!

In the beginning of Jehoiakim's reign, though Judea and all Syria were then under the Egyptian Empire, the Prophet Jeremiah, in his 27th chapter (22), foretold

(22) ——" In the beginning of the reign of *Jehoi-*
" *akim* the Son of Josiah King of Judah, came this
" word unto Jeremiah from the Lord, saying, Thus
" saith the LORD (or the LORD said) to me; make
" ye Bonds and Yokes, and put them upon thy Neck,
" and send them to the King of Edom," &c. The
learned Dr. Lowth (Prebendary of Winchester in 1718)
in his Commentary on this place, supposes that the
Name of " Jehoiakim *has crept into the Text*," &c.
" instead of Zedekiah." " This emendation" (says
he) " is confirmed by comparing this verse with the
" 3d, 12th, and 20th verses of this chapter, and with
" the beginning of the next."—But these verses, however,

foretold *the universal Empire of* " Nebu-
" chadnezzar King of Babylon," even
before

ever, are far from confirming the proposed emendation: all that can properly be said of them in this respect is, that they have occasioned, in some Writers, the supposition of an Error in the Text, which has been very well answered by others. But there is a better evidence in favour of the Doctor's supposition than what he has mentioned, because the latter really contains no difficulty, if the 3d and 6th verses be considered as *prophecies* [*] of the future reigns of *Zedekiah* and *Nebuchadnezzar:* but the evidence, which he has *not* mentioned, leaves much more room for the supposition of a various reading in the Text; for the *Syriac Version* has really the reading which that learned Gentleman supposes to be the true one, viz. ܒܪܝܫܝܬ ܡܠܟܘܬܗ ܕܨܕܩܝܐ — " in the " beginning of the reign of *Tsedekia*," instead of " in
" the

---

[*] " These things" (says the learned *Lightfoot*) " are to be un-
" derstood to be spoken *prophetically* concerning *Zedekiah*, as
" well as concerning *Nebuchad-nezzar*'s Sonnes; for the Lord
" by the Prophet foretells that *Nebuchadnezzar* should reigne,
" and his Sonne and Grandchilde after him; and therefore must
" the Prophet presently make Yokes and Bonds, and put them
" of his own neck in token of Judah's subjection, which indeed
" begun in the very next yeare. And he foretells us withall that
" *Zedekiah* should reigne, and that divers Kings should send Mes-
" sengers to him, and by them should *Jeremy* send those Yokes
" to those Kings," &c. Harmony of the Old Testament, p. 149
and 150.

before that great Warrior was King of Babylon (23), his Father *Nabopollasar* (who

" the beginning of the reign of *Jehoiakim.*" This evidence certainly proves, either that the Hebrew Copy, from which the version was made, had really the reading supposed by Dr. Lowth, or else that the Translator himself thought (like Dr. Lowth) that the word " JEHOIAKIM *had crept into the Text instead of* " ZEDEKIAH," and therefore was willing to correct the supposed error in his new version: and as the latter is neither *impossible* nor *improbable*, the evidence of the Syriac Version must by no means be admitted to invalidate the present Hebrew Reading, especially as the latter is confirmed, not only by all the ancient Hebrew Manuscripts that have hitherto been collated, but also by the Targum of Jonathan, who flourished 100 years before the destruction of the second Temple, as Bishop Walton relates * ; so that his Translation is *older* than *the oldest* Syriac Version, which is sufficiently proved in the Prolegomena to the Polyglott Bible by the same learned Bishop. The *whole verse* is wanting in the *Greek Version,* so that no evidence can be drawn from thence.

(23) Which was not till the latter end of the third year of Jehoiakim; for part of the third and part of the fourth years of Jehoiakim were included in the
first

---

* " Floruit hic centum annis ante Templi secundi vastatio-
" nem, ut habetur in Talm. Tract. de Sabbato, c. 1."—In Biblia Polyglotta Prolegom. p. 84.

(who was also called *Nebuchodonosor* (24) being still alive. The Prophet was directed

first year of Nebuchadnezzar. Compare Dan. i. 1. with Jer. xxv. 1. This was the earliest computation (there being two) of Nebuchadnezzar's reign ; for Dean *Prideaux* remarks, that " *Daniel* begins his " computation from the time that *Nebuchadnezzar* was " sent from Babylon by his Father on this expedition" (for he is speaking of Nebuchadnezzar's success in recovering *Syria* and *Palestine* from Pharaoh-Nechoh) " which" (says he) " was in the latter end of the third " year of Jehoiakim," &c. (See Connections, part I. p. 63.) " But, according to the Babylonians, his " reign is not reckoned to begin till after his Father's " death, which happened two years afterwards ; and " both computations being found in Scripture, it is " necessary to say so much here for the reconciling of " them." *Ibid.* p. 60.

(24) The learned Archbishop *Usher* shews, that *Nabuchadonosor* was a name given to *Saosduchinus*, the Successor of Esarhaddon in the Assyrian and Babylonian Empire; and that he was the *Nabuchadonosor* mentioned in the Book of Judith (See his Annals under the years of the world 3336 and 3347.) That *Chynaladan* (called also *Sarac*) succeeded this *Nabuchadonosor* in the Empire A. M. 3356: that Nabopollasar (the Father of Nebuchadnezzar), who was Commander in Chief of his Forces, rebelled against his Master *Sarac*, and jointly with *Astyages* (called also *Assuerus*),

rected to make *Bonds* and *Tokes*, and put them upon his own neck, and to send

Aſſuerus), King of the Medes, conquered Sarac, and took *Nineveh*. And it seems that Nabopollaſar at that time had aſſumed the name of *Nabuchadonoſor*, the great Anceſtor of his Maſter; for, according to Archbiſhop *Uſher*, Nabopollaſar is mentioned under that name in the Book of Tobit (A. M. 3378), *viz.* " Nabopollaſarus Babylonius, à Saraco (five Chyna-
" ladano) Aſſyriorum & Chaldæorum Rege *præfectus*
" *exercitui*," (the example ſhould warn Monarchs againſt the keeping of great Standing Armies) " &
" Aſtyages à Patre Cyaxare Mediæ Satrapa conſtitu-
" tus, affinitatem ineuntes (Amyiti Aſtyagis Filiâ
" Nebucadneſari Filio Nabopollaſari deſponſatâ)
" junctis viribus Niniven, & in eâ *Saracum* Regem,
" expugnant: quemadmodum ex Alexandri Polyhiſ-
" toris fragmento (à Cedreno, qui illud citat, minimè
" intellecto) colligimus. Quomodo & in fine Græci
" Tobiti legimus; cœpiſſe Niniven NABUCHOD-
" ONOSORUM (five *Nabopollaſarum*) & ASSUE-
" RUM (five *Aſtyagen, Aſſueri* quoque nomine, Da-
" nielis ix. 1. appellatum:) Superſtite adhuc Tobiâ
" juniore qui, capta Samariâ à *Salmanaſare*, in Aſſy-
" riam cum Patre deportatus, annis 127 (vel 99, ut
" habet Latina, ex Chaldaico expreſſa editio) vixiſſe
" dicitur," *&c.*—So that Tobit had the ſatisfaction to ſee *God's Vengeance* executed upon that mighty Inſtrument of God's Wrath the Aſſyrian Empire, which had enſlaved and carried away his Countrymen the Iſraelites from their ancient Inheritance.

them

them afterwards to the Kings of several neighbouring Nations, with a most awful message from God concerning the rising power of the Babylonian Monarch:—" And now" (said the Prophet, in the Name of the Lord, or *Jehovah*, of Hosts, the God of Israel, see ver. 4.) " have I
" given all these Lands into the hand
" of Nebuchadnezzar *the King of Ba-*
" *bylon, my Servant;*" &c.—" and all
" Nations" (many of whom are expressly mentioned in the third verse)
" shall serve HIM, and his SON, and
" his SON's SON, until the very time
" of his Land come" (for the Empire continued for *three lives* or *successions,* until the Babylonian measure of iniquity and oppression was fulfilled in the reign of Belthazar (25), when the *Medes* and *Persians*

(25) The several Histories cited by the learned Grotius, in the 16th Sect. of his 3d Book *de Veritate Religionis Christianæ,* concerning the Chaldean Monarchs, are by no means well chosen for the laudable purpose

H

name, was not *King of Babylon* when the Prophecy was delivered, as I have already remarked. But after this *foreign Conqueror* had really appointed *a King of Judah*, and given him the name of ZEDEKIAH *(the very name foretold by the Prophet)*, such an extraordinary circumstance would add unquestionable authority to the truth of *Jeremiah*'s mission, and would render *Zedekiah* and his Courtiers *inexcusable* (as they really were) for rejecting the earnest and repeated Remonstrances of that Prophet (27).

This timely Prediction, therefore, in the reign of Jehoiakim, with the internal Proofs which it contained, concerning the necessity of *Zedekiah*'s Submission

---

(27) If this probable confirmation of the word of Prophecy be duly considered, it will add much to the weight of the Observations which I have made in a preceding Note concerning the Truth of the Hebrew Text in the 1st verse of this chapter.

to the Babylonian Yoke, seems to have been absolutely necessary to enable the Prophet to confute the many *false Prophets, Diviners, Dreamers, &c.* (see 9th verse) who were (afterward, in *Zedekiah*'s reign) publickly employed to excite the People to shake off *the Babylonian Yoke.*

The Prophet was also forewarned in the beginning of Jehoiakim's reign (as the same chapter testifies) that the Kings of Edom, Moab, Ammon, Tyre, and Zidon would send Messengers to a " *Zedekiah* King of Judah;" all which Kings (as Grotius remarks) (28) were subdued by Nebuchadnezzar; and therefore it is not improbable that the said Messengers or Ambassadors were sent to *Zedekiah* for the purpose of forming

(28) Omnes enim hi Reges subjugati a Nebuchadonosoro. Vide infra xlviii. xlix. Comment on the 3d verse. Annot. ad Vet. Test. p. 221.

a league

phet having not only foretold the reign of Nebuchadnezzar, and the reign of Zedekiah (*a name* not applicable to *Zedekiah* himself till the Babylonian Conqueror thought proper to give it him, so that no worldly prudence could foresee such an event), but had also foretold the very circumstance in which they themselves were concerned, *viz.* that *Messengers* should be sent to this *Zedekiah* by such and such Kings!

In what year these Messengers or Ambassadors really arrived at Jerusalem, or returned from thence, does not appear; but as the *Yokes* were, first of all, *to be put upon the Prophet's own neck*, before he was to send them to the Kings (compare the 2d and 3d verses), and as it appears that he really wore such a wooden *Yoke*, as a sign against them, in the Temple, so late as the 4th year of Zedekiah, when a false Prophet took it from

from his neck, and broke it, and thereby occasioned a further command respecting those Kings, *viz*. that the Prophet should " make for them *Yokes* " *of Iron* (31)," it seems most probable that *the wooden Yokes* first ordered had not *then* been sent to them; and, consequently, that the Messengers of those Kings had not as yet arrived at Jerusalem (for, undoubtedly, the Prophet would obey the Divine Command as soon as he had the proper opportunity of doing so); and as *Zedekiah* went to Babylon *in the same year* (see Jer. li. 59.) it is likely the Messengers did not *arrive*, nor he *rebel*, till the year following. Nevertheless, in that year (the fourth of Zedekiah) the Prophet declared the Message to Zedekiah himself, which he had before been charged

(31) " Thus saith the Lord; Thou" (Hananiah) " hast broken *the Yokes of Wood*, but thou" (Jeremiah) " shalt make for them Yokes of Iron." Jer. xxviii. 13.

are now sitting under the IRON YOKES of *unnatural, arbitrary Governments,* subjected to the WILL AND PLEASURE of their respective Sovereigns, instead of LAW ! And if the particular History of any, or perhaps all, of these *Nations* be carefully examined, it will not, I believe, be found that any of them were ever reduced to such a deplorable state of *national* Misery, till by *national* Wickedness, and *public* Contempt of GOD's *eternal Laws,* they had rendered a *national* RETRIBUTION strictly necessary, according to the unerring Rules of eternal Justice! All hopes, therefore, of REDRESS to *these enslaved Nations* must be vain, without a sincere reformation of manners in each Nation respectively, and without *public* and most earnest *national* or *general* endeavours to obtain *Reconciliation and Forgiveness from* THE KING OF KINGS; as nothing but *a strict Obedience to* HIS LAWS *can render any*

any Nation truly FREE. Jeremiah made the same declaration also to the *Priests* and *People* that he had made to the *King* :—" Also I spake" (says he) " to
" *the Priests*, and to *all the People*, say-
" ing, Thus saith the LORD ; Hearken
" not to the words of your *Prophets*
" that prophesy unto you, saying, Be-
" hold, the Vessels of the Lord's House
" shall now shortly be brought again
" from Babylon ; for they *prophesy a*
" *Lye* (32) unto you. Hearken not
" unto them : *serve* the King of Baby-
" lon, and *live*. Wherefore should
" this City be laid waste ?" Jer. xxvii. 16, 17.

(32) These lying Prophets were probably bribed to favour the proposed *league* against Babylon, as some other wicked *Prophets* had been on former occasions, according to the testimony of the Prophet Micah :—
" And the Prophets thereof" (speaking of Jerusalem) " *divine for money*." Micah iii. 11. And *Nehemiah* also mentions a Prophet (one *Shemaiah*) who was *hired* to prophesy against him ; — " for Tobiah and " Sanballat had hired him." Nehem. vi. 10 to 12.

The

broken, as I before remarked, but he alſo pointed out the lying Prophet himſelf to the public obſervation, as a notable and undeniable token, that the Prophecies of *Jeremiah* were of Divine Authority!—" Hear now, *Hananiah,*" (ſaid the true Prophet): " the Lord" *(i. e. Jehovah)* " hath not ſent thee;
" but *thou makeſt this People to truſt in*
" *a Lye.* Therefore thus ſaith the
" Lord;—Behold, *I will caſt thee forth*
" *from the face of the earth: This Year*
" *thou ſhalt* DIE, becauſe thou haſt
" taught Rebellion againſt the Lord.
" So *Hananiah the Prophet* DIED *the*
" *ſame year, in the ſeventh month.*" Jer. xxviii. 15—17. That is, he died exactly two months after the Prediction, which was made in *the fifth month* of

" phet had broken the Yoke from off the neck of the
" Prophet Jeremiah, ſaying, Go, and tell *Hananiah,*
" ſaying, Thus ſaith the Lord; Thou haſt *broken the*
" *Yokes of Wood,* but thou ſhalt make for *them Yokes of*
" *Iron.*" Jer. xxviii. 12, 13.

the

the fourth year of Zedekiah. Such Evidence, added to the former clear Tokens of Authenticity which this Prophecy of *the Yokes* carried with it, muſt render *Zedekiah* and his Courtiers totally inexcuſable for neglecting the Divine Warning, and relying upon falſe Prophets.

Thus the propriety of conſidering the former part of the 27th chapter as a Revelation in the time of *Jehoiakim* (agreeable to the teſtimony of the Hebrew Text) is rendered apparent by the particular advantages which ſuch a prior Revelation would afterwards give to the true Prophet, when he had to oppoſe the pretended Prophecies delivered in the fourth year of *Zedekiah:* and the remaining part of the 27th chapter, from the 12th verſe, wherein the Prophet mentions his perſonal Addreſs to *Zedekiah,* muſt neceſſarily be attributed

" *Congregation.*"— Upon the Trial the Prophet perſiſted in his former declaration; but at the ſame time aſſured them of Mercy and Reconciliation, in caſe they would but repent and reform: ſo that it was abſolutely in their own power (through the Mercy of God) to have averted *the impending Vengeance.* " Therefore NOW" (ſaid the Prophet) " *amend your ways and your doings,* and " obey the Voice of the Lord your " God;" (and then he adds the condi-
" tional Aſſurance of Peace) " and the
" Lord" (ſaid the Prophet) " *will re-*
" *pent him of* the evil *that he hath*

" *Earth..* So the Prieſts, and the Prophets, and all
" the People heard Jeremiah ſpeaking theſe words *in*
" *the Houſe of the* Lord." Jer. xxvi. 1—7. Thus it is manifeſt that the public exerciſe of the *National Religion*, agreeable to the *National Law*, was continued even in the beginning of *Jehoiakim*'s reign, though he was ſet up, and ruled under the authority of a foreign Heathen Monarch (Pharaoh-Neco); for the 2d verſe teſtifies, that the People out of all the Cities of Judah came to worſhip in the Lord's Houſe.

" *pro-*

"*pronounced against you.*" To this the Prophet added a short Remonstrance respecting his own case:—" As for
" me" (says he) " I am in your hand:
" do with me as seemeth good and meet
" unto you. But know ye for certain,
" *that if ye put me to death, ye shall*
" *surely bring innocent blood upon your-*
" *selves, and upon this City, and upon the*
" *Inhabitants thereof*; for of a truth the
" Lord hath sent me unto you, to
" speak all these words in your ears."
Jer. xxvi. 8—15. Whereupon he was acquitted and dismissed; for some of the Elders cited clear precedents, from the history of former times, concerning the legality of declaring *God's Vengeance* against *National Wickedness*: but though this prudent judgement of the Court of Justice saved *Jeremiah* for that time, yet it did not prevent the wicked Monarch *Jehoiakim* from murdering the Prophet's Colleague, *Urijah*, who likewise prophesied

the Prophet *Jeremiah*, in *that very year*, denounced the Judgement of God upon Jerusalem and Judea, by the hand of Nebuchadnezzar; which proves, that the City was not, as yet, taken by him; for in the fourth year of *Jehoiakim* he acquainted all the Inhabitants of Jerusalem, that—" from the thirteenth year
" of *Josiah* the Son of *Amon*, King of
" Judah, *even to this day*" (said the Prophet), " that is, the three and twen-
" tieth year, *the Word* of the Lord hath
" come unto me, and I have spoken
" unto you, rising early and speaking;
" but ye have not hearkened," &c.—

" primum statuamus incidisse in annum Jehoiakimi
" *tertium desinentem* & imprimis *quartum incipientem*;
" ita ut NEBUCADNEZAR venisse dicatur JEHO-
" JAKIMI *anno tertio desinente* vel *exacto, suo* autem *pri-*
" *mo currente*, qui respondebat partim *anno illius tertio*
" (Dan. cap. i. 1.), partim vero *ejusdem quarto* (Jer.
" xxv. 1.), propter diversa annorum initia, cum *an-*
" *nus tertius* JEHOIAKIMI & *primus* NEBUCADNEZ-
" ARIS idem principium non haberent," &c. p. 11.

" Therefore

" Therefore thus faith the Lord of
" Hofts" (Jehovah of Hofts); " Be-
" caufe ye have not heard my words,
" behold, I will fend and take all the
" Families of the North, faith the
" Lord, and Nebuchadnezzar the King
" of Babylon my Servant, and will
" bring them againft this Land, and
" againft the Inhabitants thereof, and
" againft *all thefe Nations* round about,
" and will utterly deftroy them, and
" make them an Aftonifhment, and
" an Hiffing, and perpetual (42) De-
" folations."

(42) The word עולם, here conftrued *perpetual*, does not *neceffarily* bear that fignification; for it fometimes denotes a fhorter period: fo that Buxtorf interprets it in his Lexicon as follows:—" *Seculum*," (fays he) " tempus homini abfconditum tam *infinitum &* " *æternum* quàm *finitum*, ut Gen. xvii. 8. Exod. xxi. " 6. 1 Sam. i. 22. and xiii. 13. 2 Sam. xii. 10. *&c.*" So that the words ולחרבות עולם may rather fignify fome limited term of *Defolations*—*Defolations of* (or for) *an age*, or *a certain period*, as it is rendered in the interlineary verfion of the London Polyglot Bible— " *In Solitudines Seculi.*" Buxtorf in his Lexicon remarks, that *Rafchi* and *Aben Ezra* interpret the word
L   עולם

peculiar People, he *surely* would not spare them (45)!

The 36th chapter of Jeremiah, from the beginning to the 8th verse, is next in order of date, because it relates to transactions of the same year *(viz.* the fourth year of Jehoiakim, which must be during the Siege of Jerusalem by Nebuchadnezzar, who came up in the third year of Jehoiakim). The Prophet was then directed to write in the Roll of a Book all his former Prophecies, *from*

---

(45) " And it shall be" (said God to the Prophet) " if they refuse to take the Cup at thine hand to drink, " then shalt thou say unto them, Thus saith THE " LORD OF HOSTS" (Jehovah of Hosts) ; *Ye shall* " *certainly drink.* For lo ! I begin to bring evil *on the* " *City, which is called by my Name, and should ye be* " *utterly unpunished?*—Ye shall not be unpunished: " FOR I WILL CALL FOR A SWORD UPON " ALL THE INHABITANTS OF THE EARTH, " SAITH THE LORD OF HOSTS." Jer. xxv: 28, 29. This Declaration hath been fulfilled upon all Nations of the World at different times ; and *the Sword of God's Wrath is still as active as ever!*

" *the*

"*the days of Josiah*" to that time (46). See Jer. xxxvi. 1. The Book was wrote, however, by *Baruch* the Scribe, from the mouth of *Jeremiah*, who was then in prison (Jer. xxxvi. 5. (47); and Jeremiah

(46) " And it came to pass in the fourth year of
" *Jehoiakim* the Son of *Josiah* King of Judah, that this
" word came unto *Jeremiah*, from the LORD, saying,
" Take thee a Roll of a Book, and write therein all
" the Words that I have spoken unto thee against
" *Israel*, and against *Judah*, and against *all the Na-*
" *tions*, from the day I spake unto thee, from the days
" of Josiah, *even unto this day*. It may be that the
" House of Judah will hear *all the evil* which I pur-
" pose to do unto them; that they may return every
" man from his *evil* way; *that I may forgive their ini-*
" *quity and their sin*." Jer. xxxvi. 1——3. So that
Repentance might still have prevented " *all the evil.*"

(47) " Then Jeremiah called *Baruch* the Son of
" *Neriah:* and *Baruch* wrote from the mouth of *Jere-*
" *miah* all the Words of the Lord, which he had spoken
" unto him, upon a Roll of a Book. And *Jeremiah*
" commanded *Baruch,* saying, *I am shut up; I cannot*
" *go into the House of the Lord:* therefore go thou, and
" read in the Roll which thou hast written from my
" mouth, the Words of the LORD, in the ears of the
" People in the LORD's House, upon the *Fasting*
" *Day:*" &c. Jer. xxvii. 4—6.

This

he afterwards affigns them another date with more certainty. And to the fame year (the fourth of Jehoiakim) that learned Prelate alfo places the 35th chapter, concerning the *Rechabites* (50); for, with good reafon, he fuppofes that the circumftances therein related (concerning their refufal to drink the Wine which the Prophet had fet before them by God's command) were tranfacted during the time of the Siege by *Nebuchadnezzar*, for fear of whom the *Rechabites* had taken fhelter in the City.

In the ninth month (51) of the fame year (two months after Baruch had read the

(50) "—ingreffi funt Hierofolyma, Jer. xxxv. 11. "Ubi, quum de tempore præfente dicant; *ita confide-* "*mus Hierofolymis:* colligimus capitis hujus hiftoriam "de vino a *Rechabitis* recufato, eo tempore fuiffe gef- "tam, quo Urbs à *Nebuchadnefare* fuit obfeffa." (Dan. i. 1.) *Ibid.* ad A. M. 3398. p. 120.

(51) "In manum Nebuchadnefaris tradidit Domi- "nus Jehoiakimum Regem Judæ, cum parte Inftru- "mentorum Domûs Dei [Dan. i. 2.], *menfe videlicèt* "*nono,*

the Roll of Prophecy in the Temple, which was in the seventh month) Jerusalem was taken (52) by Nebuchadnezzar,

" *nono five Cisleu* : ut colligitur ex aniverfario jejunio,
" quod in memoriam, ut videtur, hujus calamitatis
" (more apud Judæos recepto; Zachar. vii. 3, 5. &
" viii. 19.) eo menfe obfervatum eft [Jerem. xxxvi.
" 9.]." Ad A. M. 3398, p. 120.

(52) *Jofephus* feems to have been defirous to conceal this fact from his *Gentile* Readers (notwithftanding that the *Jews* held a folemn Faft in the *ninth month*, in commemoration of this *National* Calamity, in the fourth year of Jehoiakim); for he mentions nothing of the Capture of Jerufalem, but only informs us, that in the fourth year of Nebuchadnezzar, and the eighth of Jehoiakim (in which he makes a miftake of four years), the Babylonian made war with great power, demanding tribute of *Jehoiakim*, or threatening to fight him; and that the other, fearing the threats of the Babylonian, and purchafing peace with money, paid him the tributes which he had demanded *for three years*.
" Τεσσαρα δε ετη βασιλευονίος ηδη τε Ναβεχοδονοσορε,
" ογδοος ην τω Ιωακιμω τω των Εβραιων εχονίι την αρχην,
" και στρατευει μετα πολλης δυναμεως επι τες Ιεδαικς ο
" Βαβυλωνιος, φορες αιτων τον Ιωακιμον, η πολεμησειν
" απειλων· ο δε δεισας την απειλην, και την ειρηνην αυτι-
" καταλλαξαμενος των χρηματων, ηνεγκεν αυτω φορες, ες
" εταξεν επι ετη τρια." Ant. Jud. Lib. x. c 7. p. 336.

from taking more (56), or rather, perhaps, inclined him to leave the rest, that the Service of the Temple might be still continued, which it certainly was, as well as the *National Laws and Customs*, and also a *National* Prince *of the House of David* " upon *the Throne of David*," notwithstanding that the Government was then held under the authority of a *foreign Heathen Monarch*; which was the fifth (if not the sixth) time (56) that the like extraordinary circumstances were fulfilled since the promise was made to King David that his *House* and

---

(56) The reason of my speaking dubiously, whether this was the fifth or sixth time that Jerusalem was taken since the promise to David, is, because I cannot produce sufficient authorities to prove that it was taken when King *Manasseh was carried away captive by the King of Assyria*, though it is very probable that the City was then also really taken, because Manasseh, after his restoration, thought it necessary to build walls, and add new fortifications to different parts of the City. See 2 Chron. xxxiii. 14.

Kingdom

Kingdom should be *established.* See 2 Sam. vii. 11—29.

In the *fifth* year of Jehoiakim (tho' the *first* year of his Vassalage to Babylon), in the ninth month, a Fast was proclaimed, in remembrance of God's Judgements in the preceding year (57) upon

---

(57) ——" in memoriam, ut videtur, *Urbis* eodem " superioris anni mense *a caldæis captæ.*" Archbishop Usher, ad A. M. 3399. Dean Prideaux says that the *Fast* was held on *the eighteenth day of the ninth month,* and is still kept by the Jews. He also supposed (as well as Archbishop Usher) that *the City was then taken by the Chaldæans:* but see his words at length—" The " great Fast of the Expiation, wherein Baruch read " the Roll, as is above related, was annually kept by " the Jews on the tenth day of the month *Tizri,* which " answers to our *September.* Immediately after that " Nebuchadnezzar invaded Judæa; and *having laid " siege to Jerusalem, made himself master of it in the ninth " month,* called *Cisleu* (which answers to our *November),* *on the eighteenth day of that month* (for on that " day is still kept by the Jews an annual Fast in com- " memoration of it even to this day); and having " then taken *Jehoiakim* prisoner, he put him in chains " to carry him to Babylon. But he having humbled
" himself

ral different Nations (60), then subject to the Dominion of *Nebuchadnezzar*, which, under the Providence of God, were to execute *the Divine Vengeance* upon the Jewish Nation (agreeable to the express terms of God's Covenant) for having neglected *the Divine Law* (the People being at that time notoriously *corrupt and wicked*), but more particularly for having neglected those parts of *the Law* which are *eternal, viz.* the eternal Laws of JUDGEMENT (or Justice) *and* RIGHTEOUSNESS, of which the Prophets were continually remind-

(60) " And the Lord sent against him" (Jehoiakim) " Bands" (or Troops) " of the Chaldees, and Bands " of the Syrians, and Bands of the Moabites, and " Bands of the Children of Ammon, and sent them " against Judah, to destroy it, according to the Word " of the Lord, which he spake by his Servants the " Prophets. Surely at the Commandment of the " Lord came this upon *Judah*, to remove them out of " his sight, for the sins of Manasseh, according to all " that he did, and also for the innocent blood that he " shed:" &c. 2 Kings xxiv. 2.

ing

ing them!—We have no further information from the sacred Text concerning the four remaining years of *Jehoiakim*'s reign (61); only that he "*slept with his Fathers* (62), and that JEHOIACHIN

(61) For "*he reigned eleven years in Jerusalem.*" 2 Kings xxiii. 36.

(62) "It appears by this" (says the learned Bishop Patrick) "that *to sleep with one's Fathers* signifies no
"more than *to* DIE, *as they did*. For *Jehoiachim* was
"NOT *buried with them*, NOR *died in his bed:* but
"being taken by the *Chaldæans*, he died *as they led
"him out of* JERUSALEM; and, according to the
"Prophecy of Jeremiah (xxii. 18, 19.), they cast him
"out of the Gates, and he had burial of an Ass; that
"is, lay upon the ground unburied. Abarbinel
"thinks" (continues the Bishop) "he *died in the way
"to Babylon*; and his Body was left in the Highway,
"without any care taken to inter it: but it lay ex-
"posed to the Sun by day, and to the Frost by Night.
"xxxvi. Jerem. 30." See on 2 Kings xxiv. 6.

The worthy Prelate is certainly right concerning the expression "*to sleep with one's Fathers*;" for that is always mentioned as a distinct thing from *the burial* of any one: as for instance—"AHAZ SLEPT WITH HIS
"FATHERS, *and they* BURIED *him in the* City, (even)
"*in Jerusalem*; *but they* BROUGHT HIM NOT *into the*
"Sepulchres

" him prisoner in some sally (64)" (besides that it is *a mere supposition*), does not afford so literal an accomplishment of Jeremiah's Prophecy as the account of Josephus, because the words " *drawn* " *and cast forth beyond the Gates of Jerusalem*" seem to imply that *Jehoiakim*'s death should be *in Jerusalem* (as Josephus has represented it); otherwise it could not well be said that he was " *drawn and cast forth* BEYOND THE " GATES," if he did not die WITHIN THE GATES.

This second conquest of Jehoiakim by Nebuchadnezzar was the sixth (if not the seventh) time that *Jerusalem* was taken by *foreign Enemies* since the conditional promise was made to David concerning *the Establishment of his Throne*; and the Exaltation of *Jehoiachin*, by the

---

(64) Connections, Part I. p. 67.

Authority

Authority of the Babylonian Conqueror, was the *seventh Restoration* of " *the House of David*" to the " *Throne of David*," after being *as often* delivered into the hands of their Enemies for neglecting God's *Laws*; whereby the immediate interposition of DIVINE PROVIDENCE in the direction of Human Affairs is unquestionably demonstrated. But notwithstanding these examples both of *God's Vengeance* and of his *Mercy* towards " *the House of David*," the young King *Jehoiachin* (65) (alias *Jeconiah*, or *Coniah*)

(65) יהויכין is a name compounded of two words, יהו־יכין *Jehoi-achin*, or *Jehov-iχin*, signifying *Jehovah will prepare*; or, according to some, " *Domini Præparatio, sive Domini Firmitas*." (See the Interpretation of Names in the end of the sixth Volume of Bishop Walton's Polyglot Bible, p. 30.) A transposition of these two words (placing the last first) forms a name of the same import, though of a very different sound—יכיני־יהו, *Ichin-Jehov*, or *Jeχin-Jehov*: and that such a transposition of the name was frequently used is apparent, because from thence is derived, *by abbreviation*, another name of this Monarch, by which

he

Coniah) very soon afterwards fell into all the wickedness of his Fathers, and, consequently, was rejected by the GOD *of Israel*; for the Monarch was speedily informed by the Prophet *Jeremiah*, that God had determined to deliver him up into the hands of his Enemies, and into the hands of *Nebuchadnezzar, whose face he feared* (66), though, it seems, *he feared*

he is sometimes mentioned, *viz.* יְכָנְ־יָה (1 Chron. iii. 16.) "*Jeconiah*" (or *Icon-Jah*), having the same meaning with both the forementioned names, though the learned Pasor, in his Greek Lexicon of the New Testament, renders it "*præparatus a Domino,*" which is more properly the meaning of *Coniah* (כָּנִיהוּ) or *Con-Jehov* (the name by which the Prophet Jeremiah has distinguished the same Monarch, in his 22d and 37th chapters), as ו, the characteristical letter of the future tense, is omitted in the last-mentioned name.

(66) "As I live, saith the Lord, though Coniah "the Son of *Jehoiakim* King of Judah were the Signet "upon my Right Hand, yet would I pluck thee "thence: and I will give thee into the hand of them "that seek thy life, and into the hand *(of them) whose* "*face thou fearest*, even into the hand of Nebuchad- "rezzar King of Babylon, and into the hand of the "Chaldæans:"

feared not GOD! for the Text informs us that "*he did* EVIL *in the sight of the* LORD, *according to all that his Father had done.*" (2 Kings xxiv. 9.) And then immediately follows the account of *God's Vengeance* against him!—" At " that time" (says the Text) " the " Servants of *Nebuchadnezzar* King of " Babylon came up against *Jerusalem,* " and the City was besieged (67)." 2 Kings xxiv. 10.

This

" Chaldeans :" *&c.* Jer. xxii. 24—28. This chapter contains also several other Prophecies against the Sons and Successors of King Josiah, in the exact order of their respective reigns, just as the Prophet repeated them (after they were fulfilled) in his Remonstrance to King *Zedekiah* and his wicked Court; though, undoubtedly, the Prophet had before declared them in due time, whilst each of the said Monarchs remained upon " *the Throne of David :*" but no other account remains of these particular Prophecies, except in this 22d chapter, which shall hereafter be proved (I hope) to be only an occasional *repetition* of them in the presence of *Zedekiah*.

(67) The Siege, here mentioned, is erroneously cited by Dean Prideaux in his Connections, Part I. p. 67.

"This *Vengeance* muſt have followed very cloſe upon the footſteps of this King's *Iniquity*; for, it ſeems, " *he reigned in Jeruſalem*" (only) " *three months*"—" *and ten days.*" Compare 2 Kings xxiv. 8. with 2 Chron. xxxvi. 9.

" And when the year was expired " King Nebuchadnezzar ſent and " brought him to Babylon." 2 Chron. xxxvi. 10. That is, Nebuchadnezzar, firſt of all, ſent *his Servants* (*viz.* his Army) againſt Jeruſalem, who beſieged

p. 67. as a tranſaction during the life of *Jehoiakim*; whereas nothing can be more plain than the narrative of the Sacred Text, wherein, after the Hiſtorian has mentioned the commencement of *Jehoiachin*'s (alias *Coniah*'s) reign, and his evil conduct, he proceeds next in courſe to this account of the *Divine Vengeance* in the 10th verſe (which Dr. Prideaux has applied to the reign of Jehoiakim); and the Sacred Hiſtorian, ſtill continuing the account of that Siege in the following verſes, informs us, in the 12th verſe, that JEHOIA-CHIN (expreſsly by name) *King of Judah went out to the King of Babylon*, he and his Mother, &c. ſo that there is not the leaſt ground for placing the Siege in the reign of Jehoiakim.

the City (as I have already related from *the second book of Kings*) (68): but he did

(68) Dean Prideaux hoped to have folved the difficulty occafioned by his *own error* (mentioned in the preceding Note) by afferting that the Siege in the reign of *Jehoiachin* was only *a continuation* of the former Siege in the reign of *Jehoiakim*: for he fays—" After " *Jehoiakim*'s death the Servants of *Nebuchadnezzar* " (that is" (fays he), " his Lieutenants and Gover- " nors of the Provinces that were under his fubjection " in thofe parts) *ftill continued*" (fays he) " to block " up *Jerufalem*," &c. Connect. Part I. p. 68. And he once more cites for his Authority *the very fame Text* which he had before applied to the reign of *Jehoiakim*; and though he adds, alfo, the verfe which follows it as a further Authority *(viz.* 2 Kings xxiv. 10, 11.), yet neither of thefe verfes mention a word about *the fuppofed continuance of the Siege* from the reign of *Jehoiakim* to the end of *Jehoiachin*'s reign; neither can any *fuch continuance* be reafonably implied therein, to authorize fuch an affertion: in fhort, the whole error feems to have been occafioned by his adhering to his own *fuppofition* before-mentioned, *viz.* that Jehoiakim was " *taken Prifoner in fome Sally* (IT MAY BE SUPPOSED)," fays he, " *which he made upon them*," &c. (Connect. Part I. p. 67.) for which he has *not the leaft Authority*, the *fuppofition* being, on the contrary, directly oppofite to the teftimony of *Jofephus* before recited; and contrary alfo to the neceffary accomplifhment of Jeremiah's Prophecy againft Jehoiakim; which, I hope,

O has

"VITY *from Jerusalem to Babylon* (70)," and thereby afforded to all future *Administrations* of *national Government* an awful example of the *Divine Vengeance* against *Kings* and *Rulers* that neglect *the eternal Laws of* GOD! But though Nebuchadnezzar thought it necessary to depose *Jehoiachin*, as well as his Father *Jehoiakim* before him, yet he still persisted in maintaining "*the House of David* (71)" upon "*the Throne of David*," and accordingly "made *Mattaniah* his Father's "Brother King in his stead, and changed "his name to *Zedekiah* (72). This Monarch was the third of King *Josiah*'s Sons (73) that succeeded him upon *the*

(70) 2 Kings xxiv. 15, &c.

(71) Ezek. xvii. 13.   (72) 2 Kings xxiv. 17.

(73) By "Hamutal the Daughter of Jeremiah of "Libnah." 2 Kings xxiv. 18. She was also the Mother of Jehoahaz (or Shallum, as he is called in 1 Chron. iii. 15. and in Jer. xxii. 11.) the immediate Successor of Josiah, who was deposed and carried away by Pharaoh-Nechoh. *Ibid.* xxiii. 31.

Throne

Throne of David, notwithstanding that the *Nation* had been *four times* conquered by foreign Enemies since Josiah's death! But it is still more remarkable, that both these foreign Conquerors, Pharaoh-Neco and Nebuchadnezzar, should not only persist in setting up the Princes of " *the House of David*" upon " *the* " *Throne of David*," but should also remind them of their indispensible obligation to maintain the *Laws* and *Religion* of the God *of Israel* by putting upon them, respectively, a Memorial of the Sacred Name of JEHOVAH; for I have already shewn, that *Pharaoh-Neco* gave the name of *Jehoi-akim* (signifying " JEHOVAH *will establish"*) when he set up a Monarch over the peculiar People of JEHOVAH; and now again Nebuchadnezzar not only obliged his new Vassal to " *swear by* GOD (74)" that he would

(74) Compare 2 Chron. xxxvi. 13. *(viz.* —" Ne-" buchadnezzar, who had *made him swear* by God")
with

and effectually "*established for ever!*" This, surely, was far above the knowledge and comprehension of a *Heathen Stranger*, unacquainted with the revealed Laws of God!

It was also the name which, of all others, could best point out *to the Jews* the only certain method of "*establishing* " *the Throne of David,*" then newly restored (and, indeed, of *establishing every other Throne* to the end of the World); I mean a strict conformity to *the eternal Law of Righteousness,*—" THE RIGH- " TEOUSNESS OF JEHOVAH." There was no other method of averting the

" dah shall be saved, and Israel shall dwell safely: " and *this is his name* whereby he shall be called, THE " LORD OUR RIGHTEOUSNESS." (Jer. xxiii. 5, 6.) *i. e.* יהוה־צדקנו *Jehovah-Tsadecnu*, which is the same name (only transposed) with *Zidekiah* צדק־יהו, or *Tsadek-Jehov*, except that the former has the small addition of the possessive particle נו, signifying OUR, *viz.* JEHOVAH OUR RIGHTEOUSNESS, instead of THE RIGHTEOUSNESS OF JEHOVAH.

dreadful

dreadful *Retribution* at that time fully due to the *Jewish Nation!* — that impending *Vengeance* and *Desolation*, of which the Conqueror and present Restorer of the Kingdom was, himself, *the appointed Executioner* in case of *Disobedience!* See how the *same means* of averting *God's Vengeance* has been since set before us, even by THE SAVIOUR OF THE WORLD HIMSELF, as the *first principle* of sound policy :—" *Seek ye* FIRST *the Kingdom*
" *of God and* HIS RIGHTEOUSNESS, *and*
" *all these things*" (temporal necessaries)
" shall be added unto you." Mat. vi. 33. But *Zedekiah* paid so little regard to " *the Righteousness of Jehovah,*" and proved so notoriously unworthy to bear *that glorious name*, that the Prophet *Jeremiah*, was very soon afterwards, commanded to denounce *God's Vengeance* against him, even in the beginning, as it seems, of his reign, that is (as the Text informs us) " *after that* NEBU-
P " CHADREZZAR

Prophet repeats a part of the 24th chapter, relating to the Type of *Evil Figs*; which (as well as the preamble of each) proves that thefe two chapters were delivered about the fame time. The two next chapters *(viz.* xxx. and xxxi.) feem alfo to follow very properly (79).

In the beginning (80) alfo of Zedekiah's reign the Prophet *Jeremiah* denounced God's *Vengeance* againſt *Elam* (or Perfia); but promifed, at the fame time, a future Reftoration. See the 49th chapter of Jeremiah, from the

(79) I have before quoted the opinion of Archbiſhop *Uſher*, where he fuppofes thefe two chapters might *perhaps* be referred to the date of the 45th chapter; but he afterwards, with more certainty, refers them to the time of the 29th chapter (ad A. M. 3406), which is agreeable alfo to the opinion of Dr. *Lightfoot* (Harmony of the Old Teſt. p. 159.)

(80) " In principio regni Sedekiæ, Prophetia de " Elamitis tùm fubigendis tùm reſtaurandis à Jeremîâ " prolata eſt (Jer. xlix. 34, 39.)," *&c.* Ad A. M. 3405, p. 125.

34th

34th verse (81). Whether the *Judgements* against Ammon, Edom, Damascus, &c. contained in the former part of this chapter were delivered also at the same time does not appear: it is rather more probable that they were delivered about the same time with the 46th and 48th chapters, *viz.* in the fourth year of Jehoiakim; for which opinion I have already quoted the authority of the learned *Lightfoot*. Some of these Nations were doomed to *temporal Vengeance* in the beginning of *Jehoiakim*'s reign. The Prophecy of this *Vengeance* (contained in the 27th chapter of Jeremiah) was to be afterwards communicated to them, by their own Ambassa-

---

(81) " The Word of the Lord that came to *Jere-*
" *miah* the Prophet against ELAM *in the beginning of*
" *the reign of* ZEDEKIAH *King of Judah,* saying,
" Thus saith the LORD of Hosts" *(Jehovah of Armies)*;
" Behold, I will break *the Bow of Elam,*" &c. The Persians were always famous *Archers,* as well as excellent Horsemen.

dors,

"*him Horses and much People;*" so that he seems to have entertained a foolish and wicked desire to render himself *absolute* and *independent* by means of a Standing Army of foreign Mercenaries; for he not only endeavoured to procure Horses from Egypt, but also "*much People* (83)." Ezek. xvii. 15. And as he vainly put his whole trust in a *military Force*, the *solemn Oath*, which he had so lately taken, was made to yield to his *political views*, though he had called GOD *to witness!* So that the perjured Monarch's WILL AND PLEASURE was preferred to that RIGHTEOUSNESS in the execution of *Covenants* and *Laws* which *alone can establish the Thrones of Kings* (84), and of

---

(83) "Shall he prosper? shall he escape that doth such *(things)*?" Ezek. xvii. 15.

(84) "*Take away the* WICKED *from before the King, and his Throne shall be* ESTABLISHED IN RIGHTEOUSNESS." PROV. xxv. 5. — "For the Throne is established by RIGHTEOUSNESS." Chap. xvi. 12.

"IN

of which his new name (Zedekiah, or *Righteousness of Jehovah*) was certainly intended to remind him. This wicked policy was censured in the severest terms by the Prophet Ezekiel:—" *Shall he
" prosper?*" (said the Prophet) " shall
" he escape that doth such (things)? or
" shall he break the Covenant, and be
" delivered? As I live, saith the Lord
" God, surely in the place *(where)*
" the King *(dwelleth)* that made him
" King, whose Oath he despised, and
" whose Covenant he brake, *(even)* with
" him, in the midst of Babylon, he

" In righteousness *shalt thou be* established." Isaiah liv. 14.

" And in mercy shall the throne be established, *and he shall sit upon it* in truth, *in the Tabernacle of David, judging and seeking Judgement*" (or Justice), " *and hasting* righteousness." Isaiah xvi. 5. The constant lesson of the Prophet Jeremiah to Zedekiah and the House of David was—" Execute
" ye judgement and righteousness, *and deliver
" the Spoiled out of the hand of the Oppressor*—Do no
" wrong, do no violence to the stranger," &c.

" shall

also in the reign of Josiah. Compare Jer. i. 15. with xxv. 9. In the former, God declares,—" *I will call all the Fa-* " *milies of the Kingdoms of the North,*" &c. and in the latter, " Behold, *I will* " *send and take all the Families of the* " *North,* saith the Lord" (thereby marking his absolute direction of them), " and Nebuchadrezzar the King of " Babylon MY SERVANT, and will " bring them *against this Land,*" &c.

And accordingly, after Nebuchadnezzar had strengthened his Empire, by reducing to his obedience all the Kingdoms of the *Assyrian* as well as the *Syrian* Dominion (which latter lay to *the North* of Judæa, and extended quite up to *Armenia,* the *Armenians* themselves being no other than *Syrians*; for *Aram* is the proper name in Scripture for *Syria),* he compelled the conquered Nations to assist him in reducing others to a like servile fervile fubjection under his own arbitrary *Will*, without perceiving that he and they, *collectively*, were but a mere inftrument of *Vengeance* (86) in the hands of *the Lord of Hosts*, or *God of Armies!* for we read in the 34th chapter of Jeremiah, that Nebuchadnezzar literally fulfilled the former Prophecies by coming to fight againft Jerufalem, *with*

---

(86) " *And thus was* NEBUCHADNEZZAR *raifed up* " *by God, to be a* SCOURGE" (compare this with what I have already remarked concerning that Monarch in pages 67, 68, 83, and 84) " TO ALL THE NATIONS " ABOUT HIM, *for the Punifhment of their Sins.* NE- " BUCHADNEZZAR had, indeed, OTHER THINGS " IN HIS HEAD. That which he defigned, was the " gratifying his own Ambition, and enlarging his " Dominions: but thefe were not the ends which God " had to ferve by him. God made ufe of him as HIS " INSTRUMENT, AS HIS SERVANT (*for fo he calls* " *him), for the rendering to the* NATIONS *that juft* RE- " COMPENCE OF VENGEANCE *which their Sins called* " *for. I mention thefe things the rather becaufe they are* " *inftances of God's dealing with Heathen Nations, who* " *were under no particular Covenant with God.*" Archbifhop Sharp's Sermons, Vol. I. Serm. 8. intituled, " Virtue and Religion the ONLY means to make a " NATION profperous," p. 209, 9th Edition.

" *all*

akim, because a Prophecy against the latter is recorded in the 18th verse, *viz.* " Therefore" (said the Prophet, referring back to the Offences before-mentioned) " *thus saith the Lord,* CONCERN-" ING JEHOIAKIM, *the Son of Josiah,* " *King of Judah; They shall not lament* " *for him, saying, Ah, my Brother!*" &c. " *He shall be buried with the burial* " *of an Ass,*" &c.

But if we carefully examine the whole chapter, with reference to the chapter which precedes, as well as that which follows, it will be found much more intelligible, coherent, and striking, when the whole is considered as one continued Address to *Zedekiah*, reminding him of the Judgements denounced (and then, indeed, fulfilled) against his immediate Predecessors, exactly according to the order of their reigns, and expressly for the same Offences *(viz.* OP-
PRESSION,

pression, and *the Neglect of* Justice *and* Right) for which he himself, *by name*, is condemned in the 21st chapter. The only difficulty which attends this construction is occasioned by the English Translators having used the *present tense*, in the 11th, 18th, and 24th verses (where the *præter tense* would certainly have been much more proper); *viz.* " Thus *saith* the Lord," instead of " Thus *said* the Lord to, or concern-
" ing, *Jehoiakim*," &c. which latter is the literal construction of the original, and is always so expressed in the interlineary Latin Version of the London Polyglot, *viz.* " *Sic dixit Dominus:*" for though in many other places it is indifferent to the sense, whether the *present* or *præter tense* is used, yet in these abovementioned it makes a very material difference; because the Prophet is only reminding Zedekiah of the Prophecies which he had before denounced (or, at

R least,

tivity by *Pharaoh-Necho*; and the *Burthen* of the Prophecy againſt him was, that " *he ſhall return no more,*" &c. See the endings of all the three verſes wherein he is mentioned, *viz.* 10, 11, and 12, which all *end with that Burthen.* Again, it is not likely that *Jehoiakim* (who is mentioned next in order) was *then the reigning Prince,* becauſe his Son and Succeſſor *Jehoiachin* (alias *Coniah,* or *Jeconiah*) is mentioned in the continuance of the ſame Declaration, in a much more conſpicuous light than *Jehoiakim* himſelf, being addreſſed in the ſecond perſon, as if preſent at the time of the Denunciation, *viz.* " *I will give* " THEE *into the hand of them that ſeek* " THY *Life,*" &c. " *And I will caſt* " THEE *out,*" &c.

And though *Jehoiachin,* probably, was the reigning *Prince* upon the Throne, when this ſevere Prophecy againſt

against him was *first of all* denounced; and also though he is expressly spoken of, in the 28th verse, as present, *viz.* " *This Man* CONIAH ;" yet he was not the Prince that *sat* " *upon the Throne of* " *David*," when Jeremiah repeated (as I conceive) *these several Prophecies*, mentioned in the 22d chapter; because the Prophet, after a most solemn and alarming exclamation (" O EARTH, EARTH, " EARTH, *hear the Word of the Lord!*") concludes his Message with a dreadful Sentence against a Prince whom he also calls " *this Man*," as if present *(viz.* " *Write ye* THIS MAN *childless*")*, which by no means agrees with the case either of *Jehoiakim* or *Coniah*. The former certainly *was not childless*; for, besides his Son *Jehoiachin*, or *Coniah*, it is not improbable but that, " *Daniel and his fel-* " *lows*" (or, at least, some of them) were also *the Children of* JEHOIAKIM; for they were " OF THE KING'S SEED,

" AND

"*Man childless*," could not relate to *Coniah*, nor to any other Prince of the House of David, cotemporary with *Jeremiah*, except ZEDEKIAH ALONE, and *in him* it was, indeed, *literally fulfilled*; for " *the King of Babylon slew the* SONS " *of* ZEDEKIAH *in* RIBLAH *before his* " *Eyes*" (Jer. xxxix. 6.) : which clearly answers to the Prophecy, " *Write ye* " *this Man* CHILDLESS (90)." Now, as

---

(90) I have taken the more pains to explain this necessary application of the Prophecy, because, amongst the Commentators that have erroneously applied it to *Coniah*, I have to oppose the weighty authority of the very learned and worthy Archbishop of Armagh, for whose testimony, in general, I have the highest esteem, though here I am obliged to dissent from him, on account of the superior authority of the Text. He says,——" *Contra hunc*" (speaking of JEHOIACHIN) " *severissimum Dei Judicium denunciatum* " *extat in fine capitis* xxii. *Jeremiæ, sententiâ hac, quasi* " *in acta referendâ, domum conclusum.* SCRIBITE VI- " RUM HUNC LIBERIS CARENTEM, VIRUM NON " PROSPERATURUM IN DIEBUS SUIS: NAM NON " PROSPERABITUR DE SEMINE EJUS QUISQUAM " SESSURUS IN SOLIO DAVIDIS, ET DOMINATU-
" RUS

as it is manifest, that the last verse of the 22d chapter of Jeremiah was addressed

"RUS AMPLIUS IN JUDA. Jer. xxii. 30." Vide ad A. M. 3405, p. 123. This by no means agrees with the case of *Jehoiachin*, but is perfectly answerable to that of *Zedekiah*, who was not only rendered *childless* by the Sword, but was also " *a man that*" did " *not prosper in his days* ;" for he afterwards lingered out a miserable life, BLIND and IN CHAINS, at *Babylon** ! whereas *Jehoiachin*, who was carried into Captivity before him, did, after that time, really " PROSPER " IN HIS DAYS ;" for though he had done *evil in the sight of the Lord*, for which he was removed, as I have before remarked, yet the great Searcher of Hearts perceived something in him worthy of the Divine Mercy, as also in several others that were carried into Captivity at the same time, which was declared very soon *after* the commencement of their punishment, and a mitigation was then promised by the Prophet Jeremiah, under the type of " *a Basket of Good Figs*" (see the 24th chapter) : whereas Zedekiah and those who remained with him were likened to *a Basket of Evil Figs*, to which a heavy curse was annexed, *perfectly* agreeable to the severe sentence in chap. xxii. 30. which I have applied to *Zedekiah*, and *as perfectly* unapplicable to *Jehoiachin*. The latter, and those that

---

* " *Moreover*" (says the Text) " *he*" (the King of Babylon) " PUT OUT ZEDEKIAH'S EYES, *and bound him with* " CHAINS, *to carry him to* BABYLON." Jer. xxxix. 7.

chapter, is nearly a Repetition of the Anſwer which the Prophet had before returned by *Paſhur* and *Zephaniah*, the Meſſengers ſent to him by King *Zede-*

(91) I have had the ſatisfaction to find (ſince I wrote the above) that the learned *Grotius* was alſo of the ſame opinion, and that he alſo confirms what I have ſuggeſted above, concerning the *Repetition* of former Prophecies in the preſence of King *Zedekiah*; for in his Commentary on the beginning of the 22d chapter — " *Hæc dicit Dominus*" — he thus expreſſes himſelf: — " *Hæc* DIXIT" (ſays he, preferring the *præter* to the *preſent* tenſe) " JEREMIAS *enim Sedeciæ* " *loquens* SIMUL REPETIT QUÆ REGIBUS ANTECE- " DENTIBUS, *fratri ſcilicet ipſius* SEDECIÆ, *fratriſque* " *filio* PRÆDIXERAT, *ne quid haberent quod de tam* " *gravi Dei ultione conquererentur.*" Annotata ad Vet. Teſt. Tom. II. p. 207. See alſo *Critici Sacri*, Tom. IV. p. 5579. I find alſo, that the Learned and Reverend Authors of the Commentary, commonly called *Aſ-ſembly's Annotation*, have objected to this interpretation of *Grotius* (for I ſuppoſe, by their recital of *his Hypo-theſis*, that they mean him, though they have not mentioned his name); but yet they have not advanced any ſufficient arguments to confute his doctrine; neither have they removed the obvious difficulties which (if I may judge of *Grotius* by myſelf) occaſioned *that Hypotheſis*; and therefore I conclude, that theſe difficulties cannot, in any other way, be ſo eaſily explained.

kiah,

kiah, as mentioned in the preceding chapter, which will clearly appear by the following collation:

Part of the Answer of the Prophet Jeremiah, sent to King Zedekiah *by* Paſſur *and* Zephaniah, *as recorded in the* 21ſt *chapter.*	*The firſt part of the Prophet Jeremiah's perſonal Addreſs to King* Zedekiah, *recorded in the* 22d *chapter.*
"*And touching* THE HOUSE OF THE KING OF JUDAH, (*ſay*) HEAR YE THE WORD OF THE LORD; O HOUSE OF DAVID" (the Addreſs to *the whole Court*, inſerted in the Remonſtrance, is here omitted, becauſe this was a Meſſage only to "*the* "*Houſe of David*")," thus "ſaith the Lord; EXECUTE JUDGEMENT *in the Morning*, *and* DELIVER (*him that is*) SPOILED OUT OF THE HAND OF THE OPPRESSOR" (this general term, "*the hand of* "*the*	" HEAR THE WORD OF THE LORD, O KING OF JUDAH, THAT SITTEST UPON THE THRONE OF DAVID, *thou, and thy Servants, and thy People that enter in by theſe gates*; *Thus ſaith the Lord*; EXECUTE *ye* JUDGEMENT *and Righteouſneſs*, AND DELIVER THE SPOILED OUT OF THE HAND OF THE OPPRESSOR; *and do no Wrong, do no Violence to the Stranger,* "*the*

In the 10th verse the Prophet begins to recite several Predictions with which he

includes all that I have said of *Mammon*) is frequently mentioned in Scripture as downright *Idolatry:* " For " *this ye know*" (said the Apostle Paul to the Ephesians, chap. v. 5.), " *that no Whoremonger*, nor *unclean per-* " *son*, nor COVETOUS MAN, WHO IS AN IDO- " LATER, *hath any Inheritance in the Kingdom of* " *Christ and of God.*" And in the Epistle to the Colossians the same Apostle warns us against some of the common Vices which draw down the Wrath of God, *viz.* " *Fornication, Uncleanness, inordinate Affection,* " *evil Concupiscence,* and COVETOUSNESS, *which* " *is* IDOLATRY." Col. iii. 5.

Neither is *Covetousness* the only Vice that is deemed *Idolatry*—all the other Lusts and carnal Indulgences are equally ranked with *Idolatry:* so that those inconsiderate persons, who yield to any of them, may as aptly be said to " *serve other Gods,*" as those backsliding Professors of Christianity at *Philippi,* whom the Apostle Paul expressly charged with this kind of *Idolatry, viz.* " *whose God is their Belly:*" — " For " *many walk*" (says he) " *of whom I have told you often,* " *and now tell you, even weeping,* (that they are) *the* " ENEMIES *of the Cross of* CHRIST : *whose end* (is) " *Destruction,* WHOSE GOD (is their) BELLY, *and* " (whose) *Glory* (is) *in their Shame, who mind earthly* " *things.*" Philip. iii. 18, 19. And the *Service of*
the

the Belly *, is placed in as direct opposition to *the Service of Christ*, as the *Service of the Pantheon*, or *all the Heathen Deities* could be, for it is as effectually *the Service of Devils*, as the latter!—" *Whosoever committeth* SIN *is the* SERVANT *of* SIN;" (John viii. 34.) and if " *the Servant of Sin,*" then also the *Servant of the Devil*; for—" *He that committeth* SIN (said the same Apostle) IS OF THE DEVIL." (1 John iii. 8.)—And though Men are not so lost to Common Sense in these more enlightened Days of *Christianity*, as personally to worship at the Shrines of *Demons* or *Devils*, yet they serve the *Devil* as *effectually as ever* to the Destruction of their own Souls, by yielding to his temptations, whether through *Mammon* or *Carnal Lust!*——For —" *Know ye not that the* UNRIGHTEOUS *shall* NOT IN-
" HERIT THE KINGDOM OF GOD? *be not deceived*;
" *neither Fornicators, nor Idolaters; nor Adulterers, nor*
" *Effeminate, nor Abusers of themselves with Mankind,*
" *nor Thieves, nor Covetous, nor Drunkards, nor Revilers, nor Extortioners, shall* INHERIT THE KING-
" DOM OF GOD." 1 Cor. vi. 9 and 10.

Thus it is clearly demonstrable (I trust) that Mankind may be guilty of *Idolatry*, and of *serving Devils*, without paying any personal Adoration to their *Idols*; and on this I found my warning not only to *Slavedealers* and *Slave-holders*, but also to my Countrymen

---

* Even the Schismatical Teachers of Novel Doctrines are ranked with those *Idolaters* who " *serve their own Belly*, and serve not " God."—" *For they that are such* SERVE NOT *our Lord* JESUS " CHRIST, *but* THEIR OWN BELLY ; *and by good words and* " *fair speeches deceive the hearts of the simple.*" Rom. xvi. 18.

their *Royal Dignity*, and were carried away thofe Regions, though they muft take notice that their reformation is but half compleat, and confequently that they are ftill in danger, whilft they permit individuals to hold in perpetual *Bondage* * the poor African Captives already imported. Now if we confider what " *multitudes of men* muft have been
" *killed* merely in the attempt to take fo many wretch-
" ed Captives for fale; and again *what multitudes*,
" out of fo large a number, would *die*, as ufual, in
" their paffage to the Weft Indies and America either
" of Grief and Defpair, or by being inhumanly ftifled
" in the Holds of Ships; befides the large proportion
" (nearly one half) that would *die* of the feafoning,
" (as it is called) after their arrival in the planta-
" tions; and laftly that all the remainder of *this vaft*
" *multitude of* 104,100 *miferable human beings* will
" probably be *worn out* by hard fervice and oppreffion
" in the fpace of about 16 years, or lefs, according
" to the average rate of fome calculations that have
" been publifhed. Thefe confiderations, I fay, muft
" needs infpire us with indignation and horror even
" though the evil, at prefent, is at a confiderable dif-
" tance from us." See the Appendix to my " Re-
" prefentation of the Injuftice and Dangerous Ten-
" dency of *Tolerating Slavery*, &c."

Add to this Deftruction the number of brave Seamen that are annually cut off, either by the Rifing of

---

* See *the Vengeance of God* denounced by the Prophets *Ifaiah* and *Jeremiah* againft the mighty Babylonian Empire and it's Monarch, " *which opened not the Houfe of his Prifoners*" (Ifa. xiv. 17.), but *oppreffed* the Captives they had taken, and " *held them* " *faft*; THEY REFUSED TO LET THEM GO." Jer. l. 33.

away *in chains* before him into a slavish Captivity,

the Negroes * in the Slave Ships, or by pestilential distempers caught from the poor Negroes confined in the holds of the said ships; add also the number of free Negroes occasionally blown up †, and otherwise murdered and destroyed by the inhuman Commanders of these *Slave-Ships*, as well as by the arbitrary Governors on the *Slave-Coasts* ‡; and likewise the number of poor wretches annually sent out by the African

---

* ——" *A French Slaving Ship* having been surprized by an "*insurrection of the Negroes*, who MURDERED MOST PART "OF THE CREW, the Mate, finding no possibility to escape "the like fate, had set fire to the Powder-room, and blew up "the Vessel, with upwards of two hundred Slaves on board." Gazetteer, April 16, 1773. I have heard of many instances of the like disasters happening to Crews of *English Slaving Ships*; and even one of my own Relations perished in the same unlawful Trade, with the whole Ship's Crew.

† ——" The Polly, Captain Walsh, a Ship belonging to Mr. "Adams, struck on the Bar of Bonny this last year" (the Book was printed in 1772), "and was soon after attacked by the Ne-"groes. The Captain, finding he could not save his Ship, sent "his Boat's Crew off, shut himself up in his Cabin, and when "the King of Bonny and all his People were got on board, to "the amount of *fifteen hundred and upwards*, set fire to the Pow-"der; and, Sampson like, at his death punished the treachery "of his Assailants." Treatise upon the Trade from Great Britain to Africa, by an African Merchant, Appendix F, p. 34. A deplorable *Hardness of Heart* seems to have possessed this African Merchant; for it appears, by his manner of relating the above Story, that he approved of Captain Walsh's *diabolical* deed, and esteemed it rather as an act of *Heroism!*

‡ In the year 1767, Mr. Grosile " burned the Town of An-"namaboe, and killed three or four of the Townspeople." Ibid. p. 100.

Company

Brother SHALLUM (93) in particular, as well as the principal caufe of it, the Prophet reprefented to him in very ftriking terms:—" *Weep ye not* " *for the Dead*" (fays he, meaning JOSIAH), " *neither bemoan him* (94): " (but) deftruction of the Human Species which is annually occafioned by this Curfed Trade was to be fully and fairly eftimated, it would appear enormous and fhocking! it would appear that many more unfortunate *human beings* are annually SACRIFICED to MAMMON, in the confequences of that iniquitous trade, than were ever offered up by the *Philiftines* and other deluded votaries of *Baal, Moloch, Hercules,* &c.! So that the HUMAN SACRIFICES *offered up to* MAMMON *by the* BRITISH NATION are undoubtedly more grateful to SATAN than thofe of the ancient Heathens, becaufe they are more numerous—more banefully deftructive to the Human Species! How then (if all thefe points be confidered) fhall our wretched *Slave-dealers* and *Slave-holders* perfuade the world and themfelves, that " *they have not broken the Covenant and ferved other* " *Gods!*"

(93) SHALLUM, alias JEHOAHAZ, (See 2 Chron. xxxvi. 1.) who was *depofed, put in bonds, and carried away Captive* by PHARAOH NECHO into Egypt. (Compare 2 Kings xxiii. 31, &c.)

(94) The Prophet here refers to the long mourning and lamentations which were continued for many years

"(but) *weep sore for him that* GOETH AWAY; *for* HE SHALL RETURN NO MORE, NOR SEE HIS NATIVE COUNTRY. *For thus saith the Lord touching* SHALLUM *the Son of* JOSIAH *King of Judah, which reigned instead of* JOSIAH *his Father, which went forth out of this place;* HE SHALL NOT RETURN THITHER *any more: but he shall* DIE *in the place whither they have* LED HIM CAPTIVE, *and shall see this Land no more!*" And then the Prophet immediately refers us to the principal Causes of God's Severity against the Royal House: "*Wo unto him*"

---

years in remembrance of the death of the great and good King JOSIAH, the Father of SHALLUM as well as of ZEDEKIAH himself.—See 2 Chron. xxxv. 25. "*And all Judah and Jerusalem* MOURNED *for Josiah,* "*and Jeremiah* LAMENTED *for* JOSIAH: *and all* "*the singing-men and the singing-women*" (the minstrells of those ancient days) "*spake of* JOSIAH *in* "*their* LAMENTATIONS TO THIS DAY, *and made* "*them* AN ORDINANCE IN ISRAEL: *and behold they* "*are written in the* LAMENTATIONS."

U (says

(says he) "*that buildeth his House by* UNRIGHTEOUSNESS, *and his Chambers by* WRONG; (that) USETH HIS NEIGHBOUR'S SERVICE WITHOUT WAGES, AND GIVETH HIM NOT FOR HIS WORK" (a clear description of the abominable wickedness of Slavery); "*that saith, I will build me a wide House and large Chambers, and cutteth him out Windows; and* (it is) *cieled with Cedar, and painted with Vermilion.*" For the Monarch [but *whether* SHALLUM *or* JEHOIAKIM *is not clearly declared* (95)] was more careful, it seems, to display all

---

(95) COMMENTATORS in general have supposed that the Oppression and Injustice of JEHOIAKIM is here referred to by the Prophet; but as SHALLUM, also, "*did Evil in the sight of the Lord,*" (2 Kings xxiii. 32.) it is not improbable that *both* these monarchs might have been guilty of *similar Oppression*, and that the Crime of *Shallum* might have been thus represented to *Jehoiakim*, as a warning to *himself*, when this prophecy was *first of all* delivered, soon after *Shallum* was carried into captivity: nevertheless it is only introduced

all the Elegances and Ornaments of *Architecture and the other polite Arts* in fumptuous Buildings, &c. than he was to maintain the Laws of Equity and *Natural Right!* but the Prophet adds —" SHALT THOU REIGN, *becaufe thou*
" *clofeft* (thyfelf) *in Cedar? Did not thy*
" *Father eat and drink, and* DO JUDGE-
" MENT *and* JUSTICE, (and) THEN (it
" was) *well with him* (96)? *He judged*
" *the Caufe of the Poor and Needy: then*
" (it was) *well* (with him: was)
" *not*

introduced in this 22d Chapter *as a reproach* made in the prefence of *Zedekiah*, which, I hope, I have already proved.

(96) But *no longer!* for as foon as *Jofiah* had undertaken an *unjuft war* againft Pharaoh Necho (who previoufly warned him of the folly and injuftice of it) God gave *him and his people* (who were wicked enough to concur with him in his unlawful enterprize) into the hands of their enemies upon the very firft encounter.—See the text at large, " Necho, King of Egypt,
" came up to fight againft Charchemifh by Euphra-
" tes" (then, probably, belonging to the Affyrian empire): " and Jofiah went out againft him. But he"
(Necho)

" *not this to know me ? faith the Lord,*
" *But thine Eyes and thine Heart are not*
" but

(Necho) " sent Ambassadors to him, saying, What
" have I *to do with thee*, thou King of Judah ?—*I come*
" *not against thee this day, but against* the house where-
" with I have war: for God commanded me to make
" haste: forbear thee from (meddling with) God,
" who (is) with me, *that he destroy thee not.* Ne-
" vertheless, Josiah would not turn his face from
" him, but disguised himself that he might fight with
" him, and hearkened not unto the words of Necho
" from the mouth of God, and came to fight in the
" valley of Megiddo. And the archers shot at King
" Josiah: and the King said to his servants, Have me
" away; for I am sore wounded. His servants there-
" fore took him out of that chariot and put him into
" the second chariot that he had; and they brought
" him to Jerusalem, and *he died*, and was buried in
" one of the sepulchres of his fathers." 2 Chron.
xxxv. 20 to 24. See also Esdras i. 25, &c. This
judgement against Josiah for *undertaking an unjust war* is the more remarkable, because God had promised him (by Huldah the Prophetess) that he " *should*
" *be gathered to his grave in peace,*" &c. (2 Chron.
xxxiv. 28.) but the promise was plainly conditional—
God does not deprive men of their *free will*—Josiah
had it absolutely in his own power, to have availed
himself of the promise by persisting *in Righteousness*;
God did not bring the evil upon him; nothing but
his own *Royal will and pleasure* in commencing an
unjust war, against which he was even expresly warned!

" *but for Covetousness, and for to shed in-*
" *nocent Blood, and for* OPPRESSION,
" *and for* VIOLENCE *to do* (it). *There-*
" *fore*" (that is, for all these aggravating circumstances of Tyranny) " *thus*
" SAID *the* LORD *concerning Jehoiakim*
" *the Son of Josiah King of Judah*" (and
not *thus saith*; for the present tense is
not proper in this place); " *they shall*
" NOT LAMENT *for him, saying, Ah,*
" *my Brother! or Ah, Sister! they shall*
" *not lament for him,* (saying,) *Ah, Lord!*
" *or Ah,* HIS *Glory!*" (according to the
general Lamentations that had been

ed! The promise; however, through the mercy of God, may nevertheless be said to have been fulfilled. For when Josiah was worsted before Necho, the conqueror did not pursue his advantage over the wounded monarch to prevent his escape from the field of battle, as might *naturally* have been expected on such an occasion, nor continued the war till more than three months afterwards; which circumstance may certainly be esteemed providential; so that Josiah was carried to Jerusalem, and may truly be said to have died in peace, surrounded by his friends, and was buried with the most solemn Royal Pomp in the sepulchre of his fathers.

made

" *Land which they know not?*" (for he plainly speaks of their being *cast out* as an event already past; " *wherefore are they cast out?* &c.) And if we consider the question as being put to ZEDEKIAH, the then reigning Monarch, it contains great severity: for if ZEDEKIAH had consideration enough left to reflect " *wherefore* CONIAH *and his Seed were cast out*," he must necessarily be struck with the Justice of his own Condemnation, which the Prophet was about to pronounce, with a most awful and alarming introduction:——" O
" Earth! Earth! Earth! Hear the
" Word of the Lord. *Thus saith the*
" *Lord*; WRITE YE THIS MAN CHILD-
" LESS, *a Man* (that) *shall not prosper in*
" *his days: for no Man of his Seed shall*
" *prosper*, SITTING UPON THE THRONE
" OF DAVID, *and ruling any more in*
" JUDAH."

Had

Had Zedekiah been much more abandoned than he really was, yet these dreadful Judgements, so solemnly pronounced in his own House, or *Palace*, and even before the *whole Court*, could not well have failed to affect him for the present. The following chapter seems likewise to have been delivered at the same time, in the presence of ZEDEKIAH *and his whole Court*, and was, probably, a part of the *Remonstrance* (99): for after declaring "Wo" to the wicked " PASTORS (100)" (probably meaning the

---

(99) Though the learned Archbishop Usher attributes to the 22d Chapter a different date from that which I suppose to be the true one, and applies the severe sentence at the latter end of it (viz. *Write ye this Man childish*) to JEHOIACHIN (which I hope I have already proved to be applicable to none but ZEDEKIAH), yet he was convinced that the following Chapter was delivered at the same time with the 22d. *Hoc* tempore sequentis quoque capitis xxiii. JEREMIÆ prophetia edita fuisse videtur. Ad A. M. 3045. p. 123.

(100) " Wo *be unto the* PASTORS *that destroy and* " *scatter the sheep of my Pasture, saith the* LORD. *There-*
" *fore*

X

seems very clearly to have been intended.

" *Behold, the days come, saith the* " LORD" (JEHOVAH) " *that I will raise* " *unto David* A RIGHTEOUS BRANCH" (whereas the Royal Branch, that had just been condemned in the preceding chapter, was most UNRIGHTEOUS); " *and a* KING *shall* REIGN *and* PRO- " SPER;" (whereas the former wretched *Kings* were pulled down from their Thrones, and carried into Captivity, for the Neglect of *Justice* and *Right*; but the promised King) " *shall* EXE- " CUTE JUDGEMENT AND JUSTICE *in* " *the Earth*" (which was the *constant* Lesson (104), indeed, to ZEDEKIAH and

---

(104). The necessity of maintaining JUSTICE and RIGHTEOUSNESS *in political Government*, as well as in *private life*, is so clearly laid down in the Holy Scriptures, that one would think it impossible that so many people, who profess to believe the revealed word of God, should nevertheless suffer themselves to be deluded.

and his Brothers, &c. and was as con-
stantly by them neglected). *In his days*"
(continues the Prophet) " *Judah shall
be saved, and Israel shall dwell safely*"
(whereas under Zedekiah their Desolation was compleated) ; " *and this is his*

deluded by the sophistical arguments of those unbe-
lievers, who assert, that *Vices* are *necessary to render
a state great and flourishing* ; and that *political Government cannot well be carried on without sometimes doing*
EVIL *that* GOOD *may come*. But these notions are so
far from being true, that the contrary is clearly demonstrable——" *Name any nation*" (says an accurate
and careful observer of the several histories of mankind) " *that was ever remarkable for* JUSTICE ; *for*
" TEMPERANCE, *and* SEVERITY *of* MANNERS; *for*
" PIETY *and* RELIGION *(though it was in a wrong
" way) that did not always thrive and grow great in
" the world; and that did not always enjoy a plentiful
" portion of all those things, which are accounted to
" make a nation happy and flourishing. And, on the other
" side, when that nation has declined from its former
" virtue, and grown impious and dissolute in manners,
" we appeal to experience whether it has not likewise
" ALWAYS proportionably sunk in its success and good for-
" tunes."* Archbishop Sharp's Sermons, 1 Vol. 8th
Serm. (intitled—" *Virtue and Religion the only Means
" to make a Nation prosperous*," which was preached
before the House of Commons, 21 May, 1690.) p.
209.——9th Ed.

" *Name*

(viz. in the ninth year of Zedekiah) that the Monarch sent Messengers to

likewise of the Prophecies in several of the following Chapters are also exactly noted in the text to be different from the time supposed by *Grotius:* as for instance—A *prior date* is expresly assigned to the 25th Chapter—it being intituled " *The word that came to* " *Jeremiah concerning all the people of Judah in the* 4*th* " YEAR *of* JEHOIAKIM *the son of Josiah King of Ju-* " *dah, that was* THE FIRST YEAR OF NEBUCHAD- " REZZAR *King of Babylon.*" And again, the two next Chapters (viz. *the* 26*th and part of the* 27*th)* though *posterior* with respect to the order of the Book, have exact dates assigned them, which are *prior* even to the 24th and 25th Chapters, for they are expresly declared to have been revealed " *In the beginning of* " *the reign of Jehoiakim,*" &c. The remainder of the 27th Chapter from the 12th Verse, which the Prophet addressed to *Zedekiah,* is as clearly to be attributed to the *beginning of* ZEDEKIAH's *reign,*—because the circumstances related in the following Chapter (the 28th) are expresly said to have come " *to pass* THE SAME " YEAR *in the beginning of the reign of Zedekiah:*" and the Letter of Jeremiah to the Captives at Babylon contained *in the* 29*th Chapter* is as clearly declared to have been wrote " *after that* JECONIAH *the King,* " &c. *were departed from Jerusalem,*" which was also " *the beginning of the reign of* ZEDEKIAH;" for the Letters were sent by ZEDEKIAH's Messengers: See the 3d Verse. So that the last mentioned supposition of the learned Grotius cannot be true.

consult

consult the Prophet, and thereby occasioned this public Remonstrance.

The War was immediately carried on with Vigour, it seems, in every part of the Kingdom (see the 34th chapter (106); and after some considerable progress had been made in it, ALL THE FENCED CITIES BEING TAKEN except THREE (see the 7th verse), the Prophet received a further Command from God relating to King ZEDEKIAH, " saying, " Thus saith the LORD" *(i. e.* JEHOVAH) " THE GOD OF ISRAEL; *Go, and* " *speak to* ZEDEKIAH *King of Judah,* " *and tell him, Thus saith the* LORD; " *Behold, I will give this City into the*

(106) " *The word which came unto* JEREMIAH *from* " *the* LORD, *when* NEBUCHADNEZZAR *King of Babylon, and* ALL *his army, and* ALL *the Kingdoms of* " *the Earth of his Dominion, and* ALL *the people* " FOUGHT *against Jerusalem, and against* ALL *the* " *Cities thereof.*" (Jer. xxiv. i.)—So that a general Attack seems to have been made at once in every part!

" hand

the most acceptable Sacrifice in the sight of a merciful God, and, consequently, the most effectual means to avert the NATIONAL DESTRUCTION, which was then advancing with dreadful strides! And accordingly we find, that he actually prevailed (108) upon his Princes and People to PROCLAIM LIBERTY *to*

(108) The Text informs us, " *that the King* ZEDE-
" KIAH *had made a covenant with all the People which*
" *were at Jerusalem to* PROCLAIM LIBERTY *unto*
" *them*; *that every man should let his man-servant, and*
" *every man his maid-servant, being an Hebrew or He-*
" *brewess*, GO FREE; *that none should* SERVE *him-*
" *self of them*," (to wit) " *of a Jew his Brother*." And
it is probable that this was the *King's own proposal,*
(though perhaps at the suggestion of the PROPHET,
to *fulfil the Law*), because in the following verse it is
said, that ALL THE PRINCES *and* ALL THE PEOPLE
HEARD *that they should let their man-servant,* &c. GO
FREE—*they* OBEYED—and these terms *hearing and
obeying* seem to imply that neither the *Princes nor the
People* were the proposers of the equitable measure,—
" *Now*" (says the Text) " *when* ALL *the Princes and*
" ALL *the People which had entered into the Covenant*
" HEARD *that every one should let his man-servant and*
" *every one his maid-servant* GO FREE, *that none should*
" *serve themselves of them any more, then* THEY OBEY-
" ED, *and* LET THEM GO. Chap. xxxiv. 8 to 10.

their

their POOR BRETHREN IN BONDAGE; and this Proclamation of LIBERTY was a public Act of the State (109); for not only the King, but *all the Princes,* and *all the People,* bound themselves, in a most solemn covenant, to comply with the terms of the Proclamation (110), which was also agreeable to an ancient Ordinance of their Law (111). Now, to confirm all that I have hitherto asserted concerning the principal causes of God's Anger against the Jews, my Readers are earnestly requested to remark, that this *material Reformation* was

(109) "COMMUNI DECRETO" (says Grotius upon the place) "*statuerat impleri quod lex jubebat,* "*sed Judæi, non observaverant.*" Vide Exod. xxi. 2. Deut. xv. 12.

(110) Viz. "That every man should let his man-"servant, and every man his maid-servant, being an "Hebrew or Hebrewess, *go free,*" &c. 9th verse.

(111) "*And ye shall hallow the fiftieth year, and* "PROCLAIM LIBERTY *throughout*" (all) "*the Land* "*unto* ALL THE INHABITANTS *thereof; it shall be a* "*Jubilee unto you,*" &c. Levit. xxv. 10.

ACCEPTED

"*turn: and brought them* INTO SUB-
"JECTION *for Servants and for Hand-*
"*maids.*" Jer. xxxiv. 11. Perhaps they thought to excuse themselves, like our *modern African Merchants* and *American Planters*, by pleading THE NECESSITY of *tolerating Slavery*, and the *exaction of involuntary Service*; *viz.* that the Profit arising therefrom was *necessary* for their support; and that Husbandry and other laborious business could not be performed at so cheap a rate by free hired Servants as by Slaves: but whether such reasons as these, or others of greater weight, were then alledged, is not material; it is sufficient for the present argument to be certain, that, whatever were their Pretences or Excuses for enslaving their Brethren, they did only *deceive themselves*, and hasten the Vengeance of Almighty God upon their own heads; for they were, very soon afterwards, delivered up into the hands of

of their Enemies, the Babylonian Tyrants, under whom their Countrymen, that had been carried away in the former Captivities, *experienced*, IN THEIR OWN PROPER PERSONS, *the deplorable condition of* SLAVES, being a moſt juſt puniſhment for that TYRANNY and *unreaſonable* VASSALAGE with which they ſo unlawfully *oppreſſed their* POOR BRETHREN! Such was their *Crime* (I mean their *principal Crime*, or at leaſt one of thoſe *Crimes* which was *moſt abominable* in the ſight of a *merciful* GOD; for they were, indeed, notoriouſly guilty of Idolatry, and many other deteſtable Crimes beſides this) and ſuch their *retaliated Puniſhment*, which was inflicted exprefsly on that account.—" THERE-
" FORE" (ſays the Text; ſo that *the reaſon* of God's interpoſition is manifeſt)
" the *Word of the* LORD *came to Jeremiah*
" *from the* LORD, *ſaying, Thus ſaith the*
" LORD (JEHOVAH), *the* GOD *of Iſrael*;

Z   " *I made*

" *hold,* I PROCLAIM A LIBERTY *for*
" *you, faith the* LORD" (significantly marking his detestation of *Slave-holding* by an ironical repetition of that opposite measure (the *proclaiming* of LIBERTY) which they had neglected; and therefore God himself PROCLAIMED a different kind of LIBERTY—LIBERTY)
" *to the Sword, to the Pestilence, and to*
" *the Famine:*" (here is a PROCLAMATION OF LIBERTY *with a vengeance!* But alas! the hardened Jewish *Slave-holders,* like *Englishmen* now-a-days, were *too wicked* to take warning.) "*And*
" *I will make you*" (faith the Lord)
" *to be removed into all the Kingdoms of*
" *the Earth*" (that is, to be led away *into Captivity* by their Enemies: SLAVERY being a very just as well as common punishment for TYRANTS). "*And*
" *I will give the men that have transf-*
" *greffed my Covenant, which have not*
" *performed the Words of the Covenant*
" *which*

" *which they had made before me, when*
" *they cut the Calf in twain, and paſſed*
" *between the Parts thereof* (115), *the*
" *Princes of Judah, and the Princes of*
" *Jeruſalem, the Eunuchs, and the Prieſts,*

(115) For in making the Covenant before God in the Temple to *proclaim Liberty*, as mentioned in the 15th verſe, they divided the victim in two parts, and paſſed between the parts in imitation of the ſolemn Covenant which God made with *Abraham*, when a ſmoaking furnace, and a lamp of fire, paſſed between the pieces of the divided Heifer, She Goat, &c. as mentioned in Gen. xv. 9 to 17, ſignifying, ſays Vatablus, —" *that they wiſh to be put to death as this Calf was* " *cut aſunder, if they break the Covenant.*"—In federe pangendo dividebant vitulum, et per medium tranſibant, ſignificantes ſe optare emori ut ille vitulus erat cæſus ſi fedus frangerent. Crit. Sac. Tom. 4. 5640. —" Nam ſignificabat" (ſays Munſter) " ritus ille ut, " ſi quis dolo malo diſceſſiſſet a pollicitis, illum quo- " que ſecaret Dominus et occideret horrendé." Crit. Sac. 5639.—And Clarius gives a part of the words uſed on thoſe occaſions, " Ordo orationis" (ſays he) " eſt, Dabo viros qui prævaricantur fedus meum, ſicut " vitulum quem conciderunt," &c. In Templo enim immolarant ritu celeberrimo diviſo vitulo per cujus partes utrinque oppoſitas incedebant, ſimulque jurabant et ſe devovabant ut eveniret ipſis ſicut vitulo ſi fedus rumperent. Dicit ergo—Dabo vos ſicut vitulum illum, &c.

" *and*

broke the solemn Covenant of PRO-CLAIMING LIBERTY; but GOD's VENGEANCE kept pace with *the Oppression* of the unrepenting Tyrants!). " *Be-*
"*hold*, *I* WILL COMMAND, SAITH
" THE LORD, *and* CAUSE THEM TO
" RETURN TO THIS CITY" (a remarkable instance of God's over-ruling Providence in the World! The haughty, self-willed, Babylonian Monarch and his Men of War perceived not that they were mere instruments in the hands of God!), " *and they shall fight against it,*
" *and take it, and burn it with fire: and*
" *I* WILL MAKE *the Cities of Judah a*
" *Desolation without an Inhabitant.*"
Jer. xxxiv.

There is no order of time preserved in the Collection of Jeremiah's Prophecies, as I have already remarked; for the two next chapters *(viz.* the 35th and 36th) contain Prophecies which
were

were delivered several years before, in the reign of Jehoiakim; but the 37th chapter relates to the same time exactly as the 34th chapter last quoted, *viz.* the times when " Pharaoh's Army was " come forth out of Egypt" (xxxvii. 5.), which occasioned the departure (for the present) of the Chaldeans. And it was, probably, in the interval between these two circumstances *(viz. after* Pharaoh was *come forth* from Egypt, and was advancing, but *before* the Chaldeans left the Siege on that account) that Zedekiah sent two Messengers to the Prophet (who was then at liberty, as the 4th verse expresly declares) to desire *his Prayers:*—" *Pray* " *now unto the Lord our God for us* ; but the Prophet's Answer on that occasion was not returned till the Chaldeans *departed from* Jerusalem, as mentioned in the 5th verse (and probably also not till after the Covenant about *Liberty*

"*People, that ye have put me in Prison* (119)? *Where* (are) *now your Prophets, which prophesied unto you, saying, The King of Babylon shall not come against you, nor against this Land* (120)? *Therefore hear now, I pray thee, O my Lord the King: let my supplication, I pray thee, be accepted before thee; that thou cause me not to return to the House of Jonathan the Scribe, lest I die there.*" And it appears that Zedekiah (notwithstanding his general wickedness) yet had no personal pique against the Prophet, but was

(119) This shews that *speaking Truth*, be it ever so severe, (provided it is not spoken for the sake of mere abuse, but for the purposes of warning and amendment) ought not to be esteemed *an Offence*, for surely no *truths* can ever be more harsh or severe than those uttered by Jeremiah against the Court of Zedekiah!

(120) For these Evil Counsellors, it seems, like true implements of the Devil, attempted by their false intelligence from time to time to make the King firm in his bad measures and wicked policy.

well

well inclined to grant his Petition, as also a daily allowance of Bread, as long as any could be procured (121).

And when the Princes advised Zedekiah to put Jeremiah to death, because he publicly exhorted *all the People* to go over to the Enemy (122), it appears,

(121) "*Then*" (says the Text) "*Zedekiah* the King commanded that they should commit Jeremiah into *the Court* of the prison, and that they should give him daily a piece of bread out of the Bakers Street, *until all the Bread in the City were spent*."

(122) Which would have been *treason to the state*, and a high crime, had not the Kingdom been actually condemned by the word of God, viz. "*Thus saith the Lord*; He that remaineth in this City shall die by the Sword, by the Famine, and by the Pestilence: but he that *goeth forth to the Chaldeans shall live*; for he shall have his life for a prey, and shall live. Thus saith the Lord; This City shall *surely be given into* the hand of the King of Babylon's army, which shall take it. Therefore the Princes said unto the King, We beseech thee let this man be put to death: for thus he weakeneth the hands of the men of war that remain in this City, and the hands of *all the people*, in speaking *such words* unto them: for this man seeketh not the welfare of this people, but the hurt," &c. Chap. xxxviii. 2 to 4.

that

These circumstances, and several others, will be found in the 38th chapter (126); but we must go back to the 32d chapter for the continuation of the History, which we there find advanced to the *tenth* year of Zedekiah's reign, the Siege being still carried on, and Jeremiah still shut up in the Court of

(126) —" If thou wilt assuredly go forth unto the
" King of Babylon's Princes, then thy soul shall live,
" and this City shall be burned with fire; and thou
" shalt live and thine house. But if thou wilt not
" go forth to the King of Babylon's Princes, then
" shall this City be given into the hand of the Chal-
" deans, and they shall burn it with fire, and thou
" shalt not escape out of their hand. And Zedekiah
" the King said unto Jeremiah, I am afraid of the
" Jews that are fallen to the Chaldeans, lest they de-
" liver me into their hand, and they mock me.
" But Jeremiah said, They shall not deliver (thee).
" *Obey, I beseech thee, the voice of the* LORD which I
" speak unto thee: so it shall be well unto thee, and
" thy soul shall live," &c. Chap. xxxviii. ver. 17 to 20.
The remainder of the chapter contains a further description of the judgements that were to take place in
case he refused to accept of the alternative above mentioned; as also an account of Zedekiah's expedient
for concealing what had passed between him and Jeremiah from the Princes.

the

the Prison. In the 3d, 4th, and 5th verses we find a repetition of some circumstances of the dreadful Vengeance *before* denounced against Zedekiah; but they are not mentioned in that place as being then repeated by the Prophet, but only as having been the cause of his Confinement. From the 6th to the 16th verse is related—the remarkable Prophecy concerning the Repossession of *Houses, Fields, and Vineyards* after the Captivity; in token of which the Prophet's Kinsman, Hanameel, was providentially sent to tender to him the purchase of a Field in Anathoth, to which he was next Heir. From the 17th to the 25th verse of this chapter is contained—the Prophet's Prayer on that occasion, wherein he most solemnly describes the *Mercy*, as well as the *Vengeance*, of God, then dreadfully approaching!—" *Ah Lord God! Behold,*
" *thou hast made the Heaven and the*
" *Earth*

Jerusalem being then begun, which was not to cease till the whole was laid desolate!), "*and hast brought thy People* "*Israel out of the Land of Egypt with* "*Signs and with Wonders, and with a* "*strong Hand, and with a stretched-out* "*Arm, and with great Terror* (131), "and

(131) For that wonderful example of GOD's VENGEANCE against TYRANNY, and of his MERCY IN REDEEMING *a Nation from* SLAVERY, was of all others the most eminent, and, consequently, the oftenest repeated in Scripture (as in this place), 'till the accomplishment of the much more *glorious redemption* from SPIRITUAL SLAVERY, the BONDAGE *of the Devil* *, (of which the former was only a Type;) when the Son of God invited all mankind to the FREEDOM *of the* GOSPEL,—to the True Knowledge of the LAW of LIBERTY for the regulation of their behaviour towards each other; giving them power " *to become the* "*sons of God* †;" and to partake even of the *Divine*

* " Forasmuch then as the Children are Partakers of flesh and " blood, he," (that is, Christ) " also himself, likewise took part " of the same; that through Death he might destroy him that " had the power of death," (that is, the Devil,) " and deliver them " who through fear of death were all their lifetime subject to " *Bondage*." Heb. ii. 14, 15.—" I beheld *Satan* as Lightning fall " from Heaven." Luke x. 18.

† John i. 12.

Nature

" *and hast given them this Land, which*
" *thou didst swear to their Fathers to give*
" *them, a Land flowing with Milk and*
" *Honey; and they came in and possessed*
" *it; but they obeyed not thy Voice, nei-*
" *ther* WALKED IN THY LAW: *they*

Nature ‡ by the Gift of the Holy Ghost §, which *is* absolutely promised to all that sincerely ask ‖ it in Christ's name *.

‡ ——" Through the knowledge of him that hath called us
" to Glory and Virtue: whereby are given unto us exceeding
" great and precious promises; that by these ye might be PAR-
" TAKERS *of the* DIVINE NATURE, having escaped the Cor-
" ruption that is in the world through Lust." 2 Peter i. 3, 4.

§ " For as many as are led by *the Spirit of God*, they are *the*
" *Sons of God.* For ye have not received the Spirit of *Bondage*
" again to fear, but ye have received the Spirit of adoption,
" whereby we cry—Abba—Father," &c. Rom. viii. 14, 15.
" Know ye not that ye are the *Temple of God*, and that the *Spi-*
" *rit of God dwelleth in you?* If any man defile the Temple of
" God, him shall God destroy: for the Temple of God is Holy,
" which" *(Temple)* " ye are." 1 Cor. iii. 16, 17.

‖ " *Ask* and it shall be given you," &c. Matt. vii. 7. Mark xi.
24. Luke xi. 9. John xv. 7.

* " Whatsoever ye shall ask IN MY NAME" (said our Lord
JESUS) " in my Name, that will I do, that the Father may be
" glorified in the Son. If ye shall ask any thing IN MY NAME,
" I will do it," &c. John xiv. 13, &c.—" How much more shall
" your Heavenly Father give the *Holy Spirit* to them that ask
" him." Luke xi. 13.

the scripture phrase) of JUDGEMENT and RIGHTEOUSNESS, which drew down GOD's VENGEANCE upon them! This was apparently THE PRINCIPAL CAUSE (let *Britain* therefore tremble for her notorious national *corruption* and *oppressions*) OF THAT HORRID MISERY WHICH REIGNED IN JERUSALEM DURING THE BABYLONIAN SIEGE. —" *They that did feed delicately are de-* " *solate in the streets! they that were* " *brought up in scarlet embrace dunghills!*" Lam. iv. 5. and again, " *They that be slain* " *with the sword are better than*" (they that be) " SLAIN WITH HUNGER; *for* " *these pine away* STRICKEN THROUGH " *for*" (want of) " *the fruits of the field.* " *The hands of the pitiful*" (or rather of the affectionate or tender hearted) " *wo-* " *men have* SODDEN" (that is, BOILED, for want of other food) " *their own Chil-* " *dren*, THEY WERE THEIR MEAT *in* " *the*

" *the Destruction of the Daughter of my*
" *People.*" *Ibid.* ver. 9, 10.

A more deplorable state of wretchedness cannot be described! These miseries increased till the 11th year of Zedekiah, when (as we read in the 39th chapter) " *the City was broken up* (132); and then was the DREADFUL VENGEANCE, so repeatedly denounced by the Prophet against *Zedekiah*, ready to burst on the Head of that *wicked Prince*,

(132) And it came to pass, that when *Zedekiah* the " King of Judah saw them" (that is, *the Princes of Babylon*, who sat in the Middle Gate, after the CITY WAS BROKEN UP. See ch. xxxix. 2, 3.) " and all the men " of war, then they fled, and went forth out of the " city by night, by the way of the King's Garden, by " the gate between the two walls: and he went out " the way of the plain. But the Chaldeans army " pursued after them, and overtook Zedekiah in the " plains of Jericho: and when they had taken him " they brought him up to *Nebuchadnezzar King of* " *Babylon* to RIBLAH in the Land of HAMATH, " where he gave Judgement upon him." Ch. xxxix. 4, 5. Compare this with the Note in page 48.

who,

Babylon, telling them from God, "*I will* BRING HIM TO BABYLON, *the Land of the Chaldeans; yet shall he* NOT SEE IT, *though he shall die there!*" Ezek. xii. 13. Now to complete this tremendous Example of God's Judgement against *the Toleration of Slavery*, I must add, that the King of Babylon SLEW ALL THE NOBLES OF JUDAH, that is, ALL that were taken at that time; and having put out Zedekiah's Eyes, as before-mentioned, he bound him *(Slave-like)* with Chains, to carry him to Babylon, where he and the remainder of the Jewish Captives (the former SLAVE-HOLDERS, whose OPPRESSION he had unjustly tolerated) became (according to the phrase of our modern *Slave-holders*) the PRIVATE PROPERTY of the Babylonian Tyrant and his Soldiers! "*They took the young* "*Men to grind, and the Children fell* "*under*

"*under the Wood* (136)"—under the heavy burthens of their BABYLONIAN SLAVE-HOLDERS. But, what is still more remarkable, the *Poor of the People* (who were, probably, the *Bondmen* and *Bondwomen*, whose Cause God had avenged by these heavy Judgements) were left at home to possess the Lands and Vineyards of their former *tyrannical Masters*; for " NEBUZARADAN *the*

---

(136) Lam. v. 13. In the same chapter the miseries of a foreign Jurisdiction are strongly delineated, —" *Our Inheritance is turned* TO STRANGERS, *our* " *Houses to Aliens. We are Orphans and Fatherless, our* " *Mothers are as Widows. We have drunken our Water* " *for Money; our Wood is sold unto us.* OUR NECKS " ARE UNDER PERSECUTION; WE LABOUR AND " HAVE NO REST," &c. A just recompence for SLAVE-HOLDERS! and again,—" SERVANTS" (or Slaves) " *have ruled over us,*" &c.—" *They ravished the Women* " *in Sion, and the Maids in the cities of Judah!* " PRINCES *are hanged by their hand: the faces of Elders* " *were not honoured.* THEY TOOK THE YOUNG MEN " TO GRIND, AND THE CHILDREN FELL UNDER " THE WOOD," &c. Such a *Retaliation* of *Tyranny* must every nation expect that promotes and tolerates *Slavery and Oppression!* Nothing but severe Repentance and Amendment can prevent it! O that my countrymen would consider this!

" *Captain*

by the King of Assyria (138); and the Assyrian Power afterwards devolved to *Nebuchadnezzar* in the Commencement of the Babylonian Empire, who had also himself, thrice before this last

" the Lord brought upon them the Captains of
" the Host of the King of Assyria, which took
" Manasseh among the Thorns, and bound him with
" fetters, and carried him to Babylon." 2 Chron.
xxxiii. 10, 11.

(138) According to Bishop Usher this King of Assyria was *Esarhaddon*, who (as he relates) annexed the dominion of Judæa to the Imperial Crown of Assyria, and carried King Manasseh to Babylon; but, upon his repentance, mercifully restored him to his Royal Dignity, though he was still to remain subject to the Imperial Jurisdiction of Assyria: and afterwards, when the whole Assyrian Power devolved to Nebuchadnezzar, in the commencement of the Babylonian Empire, Jehoiakim King of Judah, became his servant three years, and then turned and rebelled against him *; but the kingdom being again conquered a few years after, in the reign of his Son Jehoiachin, the King of Babylon carried the latter into captivity, and made Zedekiah King in his room, who also rebelled both against God and the King of Babylon, and thereby wilfully drew down those heavy judgements upon himself and the kingdom!

* 2 Kings xxiv. 1.

War,

War conquered *Judea*; and *Zedekiah*, the last Monarch before the Captivity, *reigned expressly by his* APPOINTMENT, so that his wilful rebellion clearly justified the Babylonian Invasion; and add to this, that the Assyrians (139) and Babylonians (140) were, in a very extraordinary manner, preordained and authorized by Almighty God to punish the crying wickedness of the Israelites and Jews; which surely may be alledged as a further justification of the con-

(139) " O Assyria! the rod of mine anger, and the staff in their hand is mine indignation. I will send him against a hypocritical Nation, and against the people of my wrath will I give him a charge to take the spoil, and to take the prey, and to tread them down like the mire of the streets. Howbeit, he meaneth not so, neither doth his heart think so, but (*it is*) in his heart to destroy, and cut off nations not a few;" &c. Isaiah x. 6, 7.

(140) " And now I have given all these lands into the hand of Nebuchadnezzar the King of Babylon, my servant, &c.—and ALL NATIONS shall SERVE him, and his Son's Son, until the very time of his Land come: and then many nations and great kings shall SERVE THEMSELVES of him," &c. Jer. xxvii. 6, 7.—Here is a manifest instance of *National Retribution* in kind!

(or enslaved) "THE INHABITANTS
" *like a valiant* (man). *And my hand hath*
" *found as a nest the* RICHES OF THE
" PEOPLE : *and as one gathereth Eggs*
" (that are) *left, have I gathered all the*
" *Earth, and there was none that* MOVED
" THE WING, *or opened the mouth, or*
" *peeped.—Shall the Ax boast itself against*
" *him that heweth therewith?* (or) *shall*
" *the* SAW *magnify itself against him that*
" *shaketh it?*" (Thus God asserts the actual guidance of his Providence in human Transactions, by representing the haughty unbelieving Monarchs of *Assyria* as mere WORK TOOLS in his hands), " *as if the rod should shake* (itself)
" *against them that lift it up,* (or) *as if the*
" *staff should lift up* (itself as if it were)
" *no wood. Therefore shall the Lord,*
" *the* LORD OF HOSTS" (or ARMIES, Jehovah Tsabaouth) " *send among his*
" *fat ones leanness, and under his Glory*
" *he*

" *he shall kindle a burning like the burn-*
" *ing of a fire,*" &c. Chap. x. 12—16.

And after encouraging the remnant of Israel to " *stay upon the Lord, the* " *Holy one of Israel, in truth,*" by a promise " THAT THE CONSUMPTION DE-
" CREED (141) *shall* OVERFLOW *with*
" RIGH-

(141) That is—DECREED on account of the *National Injustice and Tyranny* described in the 1st verse of the same chapter, viz. " *Wo unto them that* DE-
" CREE UNRIGHTEOUS DECREES," (i. e. make Laws that are contrary to *Natural Right and Justice*) *
" and THAT WRITE GRIEVOUSNESS, WHICH THEY
" HAVE PRESCRIBED: *to turn aside the needy from*
" *Judgement, and to take away the right from the poor*
" *of my people, that Widows may be their prey, and*
" *that they may rob the fatherless!* *And what will ye*
" *do* IN THE DAY OF VISITATION, AND IN THE
" DESOLATION (which) SHALL *come* FROM far?"
&c.—which was manifestly, " THE CONSUMPTION
" DECREED." &c.

* Laws like those whereby the AFRICAN SLAVE-TRADE is *promoted* and *encouraged,* or like those whereby MARRIAGE is *restrained;* like those also which *tolerate the Oppression* of the poor *Colliers, Salters,* and *Miners* in *Scotland;* or like those *diabolical* DECREES of UNRIGHTEOUSNESS and GRIEVOUSNESS,
which

" RIGHTEOUSNES;" (for the promises of blessings and forgiveness are generally blended with the denunciations of God's Judgements, in order to encourage Repentance and Reliance on God) the Prophet comforts the Sufferers under the present Affliction with an assurance that it shall not be of long continuance. *" Therefore thus saith the Lord God of " Hosts, O my People, that dwellest in " Zion, be not afraid of the Assyrian: he " shall smite thee with a Rod, and shall " lift up his Staff against thee, after the " manner of Egypt"* (that is, by holding them in A SEVERE BONDAGE, as the

---

(142) *In via* Ægypti בדרך מצרים) " Hebra-
" ismus, pro more, ritu Ægyptiorum. Eo modo quo
" afflixerunt te Ægyptii, sic te affligent Assyrii."
—Vatablus. [" Cædet ille quidem te baculo, suâque
" virgâ petet Ægyptiaco more]—ut olim Pharao."
Castalio.—" Sicut olim in Ægypto *servierunt*, et ab
" ea tandem *servitute* liberati." Clarius. Crit. Sac.

which some of our *American assemblies* have wickedly PRE-SCRIBED against their poor *Negro Slaves*, many of which I have particularly pointed out in my Representation against Slavery. pages 49 to 73.

Egyptians had formerly done (142): "*for yet a very little while*" (said the Prophet) "*and* THE INDIGNATION *shall cease, and* MINE ANGER IN THEIR DESTRUCTION. *And the Lord of Hosts shall stir up* A SCOURGE *for him*" (viz. the Assyrian) "*according to the Slaughter of Midian at the Rock of Oreb*" (viz. by the Militia of Israel under Gideon): "*and* (as) *his Rod* (was) *upon the Sea, so shall he lift it up after the manner of Egypt* (143). *And it shall come to pass in that day,* (that) *his* BURDEN *shall be taken away* FROM OFF THY SHOULDER, *and his* YOKE *from off thy Neck, and the* YOKE *shall be* DESTROYED *because of the anointing.*" &c. Again, in the 14th chapter, a similar Prophecy is delivered against Assyria:—" *I will break the* " *Assyrian*

---

(143) Sicut, inquit, olim aquis Rubri Maris Ægyptios prostravi sola baculi elevatione per Mosen, &c. Clarius. Crit. Sac.

" *Aſſyrian in my Land, and upon my* " *Mountains tread him under foot.*" And then he immediately alludes to the cruel *Bondage* and *Oppreſſion* which drew down the VENGEANCE OF GOD upon the Aſsyrian:—" *Then,*" ſaid the Prophet, " *ſhall his* YOKE *depart from off them,* " *and his* BURTHEN *depart from off their* " *Shoulders* (144). *This* (is) *the purpoſe*
" (that

---

(144) This VENGEANCE came upon the *Aſſyrians,* not all at once, but at ſeveral different periods, that they might have warning and opportunity to repent! One remarkable inſtance of it is fully recorded in ſcripture, I mean that ſupernatural deſtruction of the greateſt part of their army in one night after *Sennacherib* had blaſphemed God by his Captains, and preſumptuouſly propoſed to *carry away* the Inhabitants of Jeruſalem INTO CAPTIVITY: for that was expreſsly his purpoſe as ſignified by Rabſhakah—
" MAKE AN AGREEMENT WITH ME BY A PRESENT, " *and come out to me and eat,* &c. *until I come and* " TAKE YOU AWAY-*to a Land like your own Land,*" &c. at another time Pharaoh Necho was charged with the execution of GOD's VENGEANCE againſt them. (Compare 2 Kings xxiii. 29. with 2 Chron. xxxv. 21, &c.) After which time we hear no more of the ASSYRIAN OPPRESSOR, (that Monarchy being ſoon
after

" (that is) *purposed upon the whole Earth;*
" *and this* (is) *the hand* (that is) *stretched*
" *out upon all the Nations."* &c. Chap.
xiv. 25, 26.

This seems to be a declaration, that GOD's VENGEANCE against ASSYRIA for TYRANNY and OPPRESSION (145) should be a standing Example and Precedent for the Judgement of all other Nations, but more especially of *the Nations bordering on Judea*, because there

after swallowed up in the BABYLONIAN TYRANNY) so that his YOKE of course *departed* FROM OFF *the Nations he had* ENSLAVED, " *and his* BURTHEN *from* " *off their shoulders*," agreeable to the prophesy above.

(145) " Wo to thee that *spoilest*, and thou wast not " *spoiled*; and dealest *treacherously*, and they dealt not " *treacherously* with thee: when thou shalt cease to " *spoil*, thou shalt be *spoiled*; (and) when thou shalt " make an end to deal *treacherously*, they shall deal " *treacherously* with thee!" Isaiah xxxiii. 1. Here the Law of *Retribution* is clearly laid down. Commentators have generally understood this to be denounced against Assyria.

What RECOMPENCE can ye make for such an abominable affront to the Creator of Mankind as your detestable Traffic *in Slaves!* Cannot you be content with a *lawful* and *fair* Trade in *Gold-dust, Ivory, Gums, Wax, &c. &c.* which the African Coast will afford in abundance, but you must *traffic in the* BODIES *of the poor wretched Inhabitants,* to support your Luxuries, like those who gave a BOY for a HARLOT, and a GIRL for WINE! Are you a jot *more righteous,* who barter MEN, WOMEN, and CHILDREN, by hundreds together, for SUGAR and RUM! Is this your RECOMPENCE to God for all his Mercies? Repent in time, lest God should return your RECOMPENCE upon your own heads; for he has declared in this same Text)—" *If ye* RECOMPENSE *me*" (that is, in such an *unmerciful* manner), " *swiftly* (and) *speedily will I return* " YOUR RECOMPENCE UPON YOUR OWN " HEAD;"

"HEAD;" &c. And in the next verse but one, the Prophet marks the SLAVE-TRADE of *Tyre* and *Zidon* as one of the principal causes of his VENGEANCE:— "*The Children also of Judah and the* "*Children of Jerusalem have* YE SOLD "*unto the* GRECIANS, *that ye might re-* "*move them* FAR FROM THEIR BOR- "DER:" (but how much *farther* do the ENGLISH REMOVE THE POOR AFRICANS FROM THEIR BORDER!) "*Behold, I will raise them out of the* "*place whither ye have* SOLD THEM, "*and will* RETURN YOUR RECOM- "PENCE UPON YOUR OWN HEAD:" (Observe how clearly THE LAW OF RETRIBUTION is here laid down) "*and I* WILL SELL *your* SONS *and your* "DAUGHTERS *into the hands of the chil-* "*dren of* JUDAH, *and they shall sell* "*them* (148) *to the* SABEANS, *to a* "*people*

(148) This is not to be considered as a permission to the Jews to *deal in Slaves*, but only as a *prophecy* of GOD's *retaliation*

mark of GOD's VENGEANCE against oppressive Nations, viz. THE INFATUATION OF THEIR COUNCILS.) *"As* *"semble yourselves!"* (says the Prophet) *"and come all ye* NATIONS (149) *and* *"gather yourselves together round about:* *"thither cause* THY MIGHTY ONES *to* *"come down, O Lord. Let the Na* *"tions be wakened, and come up to the* *"valley of* JEHOSHAPHAT," (i. e. the valley of JEHOVAH THE JUDGE) *"for* *"there will I sit to* JUDGE ALL THE *"* NATIONS *round about. Put ye in the* *"sickle; for the Harvest is ripe: come,* *"get ye down, for the press is full, the* *"fats overflow;* FOR THEIR WICKEDNESS IS GREAT! MULTITUDES, "MULTITUDES IN THE VALLEY OF "DECISION!" &c. After which the Prophet denounces Judgement against

---

(149) In the common Translation it is rendered, " *Come all ye Heathens;*" but the original word הגוים more properly signifies *the Nations,* than *the Heathens.*

two

two of these *oppressive* Nations expressly by name—" Egypt *shall be a desolation,* " *and* Edom *shall be a desolate wilder-* " *ness*;" (and the principal reason of these judgments is also as expressly assigned) " *for their* VIOLENCE (150)
" *against*

(150) And the Egyptians " *for their* VIOLENCE," received from God a retribution in kind, which is still more awfully expressed by the prophet Isaiah, —" *So shall the King of Assyria lead away the* Egyp- " tians *Prisoners, and the* Ethiopians *Captives,* " *young and old, naked and bare-foot, even with* (their) " *buttocks uncovered to the shame of Egypt!*" Isaiah xx. 4.—A lively description this, of the extreme misery and contempt with which the poor wretched Ethiopian Captives, even to this day, are oppressed and vilified! —But by whom?—Not now, surely, by their old enemies, the Assyrians, for they, long ago, received a just recompence for their *Tyranny* and *uncharitableness,* and are wiped off from the face of the earth! and may we not expect that the Almighty will also visit the *modern Oppressors* of the Ethiopians, whose *barbarous* and *unfeeling* behaviour towards the poor naked *Ethiopian Captives* is equally notorious?——May we not expect that the Assyrians, or " *men of Nineveh,* " *shall rise in Judgment with this generation, and shall* " *condemn it!*" Matt. xii. 41. for they were previously engaged in a *just war* against the Egyptians and
F f   Ethiopians:

them.) "*But thou shouldest not have looked on the day of thy Brother, in the Day that he became a Stranger;*" (viz. in the day that their Brethren the Israelites were carried away Captives into a strange land; for it seems, that even to *be neuter*, or merely "*look on,*" like idle spectators, when the LIBERTY *of their Brethren was at stake*, would have been criminal; but the EDOMITES added to this Crime, by REJOICING at the Calamity, and joining the triumphant Tyrants;) "*neither shouldest thou have* REJOICED OVER *the Children of* JUDAH *in the day of their destruction*; *neither shouldest thou have spoken* PROUDLY *in the day of distress. Thou shouldest not have entered into the gate of my people in the day of their calamity*; *yea, thou shouldest not have* LOOKED ON *their* AFFLICTION *in the day of their calamity*; *nor have laid hands on their substance in the*
"*day*

"day of calamity. Neither shouldest
"thou have stood in the Cross-way, to cut
"off those of his that did escape; neither
"shouldest thou have DELIVERED UP"
(or rather SHUT UP תסגר or CONFINED
as in *Slavery* or Foreign *Captivity*, which
by the Restoration promised to the *Captives*, in the 20th and 21st verses, seems
to have been the case) "*those of his*
"*that* DID REMAIN *in the day of distress*.
"*For the Day of the* LORD *is near upon*
"*all the Heathen*" (that is "ALL THE
"NATIONS;" and then follows "THE
"PURPOSE" of RETRIBUTION *that is*
PURPOSED *upon the whole earth*) "As
"THOU HAST DONE, *it shall be* DONE
"*unto thee: thy* REWARD *shall return*
"UPON THINE OWN HEAD," &c.

The like PURPOSE of RETRIBUTION
was denounced against several Nations
by the Prophet AMOS, and first against
the SYRIANS—" *Thus saith* THE LORD
" *for*

" (them) *up to* EDOM:" (152) or rather (as the word הלמגיר more properly signifies)

(152) Grotius thinks that this Tranfgreffion was committed when Sennacherib invaded Judæa, and that many Jews upon his firſt approach fled to the neighbouring Regions, and that the Philiſtines, inſtead of protecting the poor fugitives, who had done them no injury, SOLD THEM *to the* EDUMÆANS, as if they had been taken in open war. " Cum Sennacheribus " Judæam invaſit, multi ad primum ejus adventum " in vicinas regiones ſe recepere, ut apparuit. Eſa. " xvi. 4. Philiſtini hos Judæos, qui nihil ipſis no- " cuerant, non ut ſupplices protexerunt, ſed quaſi " bello captos VENDIDERUNT Idumæis." Crit. Sac. Tom. 4. p. 6473. Many other commentators beſides Grotius have ſuppoſed this *Tranſgreſſion* to have been committed during the troubles occaſioned by *Sennacherib*'s Expediton; but it is not probable (*though indeed it is poſſible*) that this was the time to which the prophecy referred; becauſe, if it really was, the Prophecy *foretold* the Tranfgreffion *itſelf*, as well as the puniſhment of it; for we find that the Prophecy was delivered " *in the days of Uzziah*," whereas the Event to which they refer, did not happen till many years afterwards in the reign of *Ahaz:* there are ſome inſtances indeed of God's vengeance being really denounced againſt particular crimes even before the crimes themſelves were committed, which I ſhall ſhew when I come to ſpeak of Babylon; but in the caſe before us there is no neceſſity for ſuppoſing any ſuch anticipation, it being much more probable that the offence,

signifies] *to cause* (them) *to be shut up* (that is, in Bondage) *to Edom:* in short, it appears from thence, that they carried on the SLAVE-TRADE with EDOM, as our *Liverpool* and *Bristol* Merchants, and some at *London* (but few in proportion to the size of the place), do at present with America! But they were allowed but a short space for the enjoy-

---

offence, referred to by the Prophecy, was previously committed by the Inhabitants of GAZA after the combined army of the Philistines and Arabians had, by God's permission, subdued and plundered the inhabitants of Judea in the reign of Jehoram, as related in the 2d Chron. xxi. 16, 17, &c. to which it is referred in Clarke's Annotations. The cruelty of delivering up the CAPTIVES *to* EDOM at the time abovementioned, would be much aggravated in the circumstances of these times; for then the *Edomites* were become inveterate enemies to the Jews, having lately revolted from Judah, and during that very reign had been beaten, and many of them slain, in a pitched battle with the Jews, which rendered them the more implacable; and therefore the unnatural cruelty OF DELIVERING UP the Jewish Captives to *Edom* at such a time, must necessarily be esteemed a most heinous offence in the sight of a merciful God!

" *the* LORD; *for three Transgressions of*
" TYRUS, *and for four, I will not turn*
" *away* (the punishment) *thereof;*"
(now be pleased to remark, that though
the *Tyrians* were notorious *Idolaters*, and
very wicked in many other respects,
yet, here again, the OPPRESSION OF EN-
SLAVING THEIR BRETHREN (even of
a different Nation) was the only Crime
that God was pleased, more particularly,
to impute and point out to them, as
being most heinous in his sight) " *be-*
" *cause*" (said the Prophet) " *they deli-*
" *vered up the* WHOLE CAPTIVITY TO
" EDOM" (for TYRE was the *Philistine*
LIVERPOOL, it seems, which supplied
Edom with SLAVES), " *and remembered*
" *not the* BROTHERLY COVENANT (154):
" *but I will send a* FIRE *on the Wall of*

(154) Probably alluding to the league that was made between SOLOMON and HIRAM King of TYRE, (mentioned in the first book of Kings v. 12.) " *and*
" *there was* PEACE BETWEEN HIRAM *and* SOLO-
" MON;-*and they two* MADE A LEAGUE *together.*"

" TYRUS,

" Tyrus, *which shall devour the Palaces*
" *thereof.*" Amos i. 9, 10. (155) The
like *purpose* of God's Vengeance is next
denounced against Edom, on account of
her notorious violations also of *Brotherly
Love*; for the Almighty Father of Mankind will not see his creature Man oppressed and vilified without revenging
the affront!—" *Thus saith the Lord; for*

---

(155) By another cotemporary Prophet (Isaiah) a
RETRIBUTION IN KIND was denounced against
TYRE—" *Is this your joyous City, whose antiquity was
" of antient days?* HER OWN FEET SHALL CARRY
" HER AFAR OFF *to sojourn.*"—" (Ire pedibus suis in
" Captivitatem,", says Clarius, Crit. Sac. Tom. 4. p.
4905. that is, just as the poor slaves are now-a-days
brought down on foot from the inland parts of Africa
to the slave markets on the coasts!) " *who hath taken
" THIS* COUNCIL *against* TYRE *the crowning* (City),
" *whose Merchants are Princes, whose Traffickers are
" the Honourable of the Earth?* THE LORD OF HOSTS
" HATH PURPOSED IT," (plainly referring to the
PURPOSE which he had before declared in the xiv.
chap. 26. to be " PURPOSED UPON THE WHOLE
" EARTH,"—which I have shewn to be for the most
part a RETRIBUTION IN KIND) *to strain* (or pollute)
" *the pride of all Glory, and to bring into contempt all
" the Honourable of the Earth.*" Isai. xxiii. 7, 8, 9.

" *three*

bloody-minded Ammonites, for their horrid barbarity in *murdering the Wives and Children of their Enemies*, MURDER being a crime still more heinous in the sight of GOD than SLAVERY; because *the robbing a man of his Life* is a higher Act of *Oppression* and unnatural *Violence* than *Bondage*, it being, indeed, the *last degree of Oppression* that a Tyrant has in his power!—" *Thus saith the Lord;*
" *for three Transgressions of the Children*
" *of* AMMON, *and for four, will I not*
" *turn away* (the punishment) *thereof;*
" *because they have* RIPPED UP THE
" WOMEN WITH CHILD OF GILEAD,
" (157) *that they might enlarge their bor-*

(157) This example shews that God will severely avenge himself of all such abandoned soldiers as those who *kill Women and Children*, for we may be assured that no pretended Rules of War can justify such detestable outrages in his sight, unless they can produce an express Commission from the Almighty for that purpose, like that which was given to the Israelites against the wicked Canaanites, &c.

" *der*

"*der* (158): *but I will kindle a Fire in the wall of Rabbah, and it shall devour the Palaces thereof, with shouting in the day*

(158) Probably the *Ammonites* (like some of our Settlers and Planters at St. Vincents) coveted—"*that fine* CREAM PART *of the Country*"—about Gilead, then in the possession of their neighbours; and might perhaps stir up their public Financiers to *settle an arrangement for the disposal of the said Lands*, without the knowledge and *consent of the antient and lawful possessors*, as if the *supposed* political necessity to "*enlarge their border*" could justify ROBBERY and MURDER, by authority of Government!—Against similar crimes in Israel, the Prophet thus denounced God's vengeance! "*Wo to them that devise iniquity, and work evil upon their beds! when the morning is light they practice it, because it is in the power of their hand. And they covet Fields, and take* (them) *by violence: and Houses, and take* (them) *away: so they oppress a man and his house, even a man and his heritage. Therefore thus saith the* LORD" (JEHOVAH);—"*Behold, against this family*" (apparently meaning the *Family* or stock of that whole nation) "*do I devise* AN EVIL *from which ye shall not remove your necks; neither shall ye go haughtily:* FOR THIS TIME IS EVIL." Mic. ii. 1 to 3. "*For your hands are defiled with* BLOOD, *and your fingers with* INIQUITY:——*none calleth for* JUSTICE, *nor* (any) *pleadeth for* TRUTH: *they trust in vanity and speak lies;* THEY CONCEIVE MISCHIEF, and BRING FORTH INIQUITY!" &c. "——*and the act of Violence* (is) *in their hands. Their feet*

God is offended with any contemptuous vilifying of the *Human Body*, even *when dead*; and how much more then will he be offended with those who vilify their *living Brethren*, by contemptuously holding them in a despicable Bondage!)—" *But I will send a Fire upon Moab* (160), *and it shall devour the Palaces of Kirioth, and Moab shall die with tumult, with shouting,* (and) *with the sound of the trumpet: and I will cut off* THE JUDGE FROM THE MIDST THEREOF, *and will slay* ALL THE PRINCES THEREOF WITH HIM, *saith the* LORD." Amos ii. 1—3.

(160) MOAB was condemned also by another Prophet (Isaiah) for her want of Charity to the poor fugitives of *Israel and Judah* in a time that God had delivered them into the hands of their enemies,—" *Hide the Outcasts*" (said Isaiah in his denunciation of Judgement against MOAB) " *bewray not him that wandereth;* Let mine OUT-CASTS *dwell with thee* MOAB; *Be thou a Covert to them from the face of the* SPOILER: *for the* EXTORTIONER *is at an end, the* SPOILER *ceaseth, the* OPPRESSORS *are consumed out of the Land.*" Isaiah xvi. 4.

To these Judgements of the several Nations the Prophet now adds the Condemnation of *Judah*, lest the Jews should imagine that GOD's VENGEANCE was only to be denounced against *the Heathen Nations.*—" *Thus saith the Lord;* " *for three Transgressions of Judah, and* " *for four, I will not turn away* (the pu-" nishment) *thereof; because they have* " DESPISED THE LAW OF THE LORD," [now the Apostle Paul informs us, that " *all the Law is fulfilled in one word,* " (even) *in this; Thou shalt love thy* " *Neighbour as thyself.*" Galat. v. 14. and, consequently, the OPPRESSION OF THE POOR (of which the Jews were notoriously guilty, as I have shewn) was (next to Idolatry) one of the most heinous Transgressions of the Law, which principally drew down God's Vengeance upon them, though it is not particularly mentioned in this place]— " *and have not kept his Commandments;*
" *and*

" *who store up Violence and Robbery in their Palaces. Therefore thus saith the*

" Good, *and establish* Judgement *in the Gate, it may that the Lord God of Hosts will be gracious unto the Remnant of Joseph,*"--Thus the Israelites might have saved themselves from God's Vengeance by a timely repentance, but they were too corrupt and wicked, it seems, to take warning: for the Judgement is, immediately after, denounced on account of the said National Corruption and Injustice. --" *Therefore, the Lord, the God of Hosts, the Lord saith thus;* Wailing *shall be in all thy streets; and they shall say in all the highways,* Alas! Alas! *and they shall call the Husbandman to mourning; and such as are skilful of lamentation, to wailing. And in all vineyards shall be wailing; for* I will pass through thee, saith the Lord!"

Now let the inhabitants of Great Britain examine themselves, and enquire, whether there are not Corruptions and Injustice among them also, which may be equally liable to draw down *God's* Vengeance? Whether their Representatives in the great National Assembly, or " *Congregation of the People,*" do not annually encourage and promote the African Slave-Trade, which includes infinitely more Oppression and Injustice *than the Israelites* were ever guilty of! and whether the poor *Miners, Colliers,* and *Salters* of Scotland, who lately applied to them for relief from the monstrous Oppression and Injustice of the unreasonable Landholders (an oppression

"*the Lord God; an Adversary* (there "shall be) *even round about the Land:*

pression at least equal to, if not far exceeding the Israelitish Bondage of the Poor) have yet received *redress* for the Injuries done them? or whether, on the contrary, the *Injustice* (which never had any other foundation but that of *unjust Force* and *Usurpation*) is not now confirmed for a certain number of years longer by act of Parliament! But, O my countrymen! let us call to mind (before it is too late) the dreadful consequences of turning "JUDGEMENT INTO "WORMWOOD," and of "*leaving off Righteousness* "*in the Earth!*" Let us remember the heavy Judgements that are denounced against the *Oppressions of the poor,* and that there is ONE who will surely avenge their cause,—"THE LORD (JEHOVAH) *is* HIS NAME "*that strengtheneth the* SPOILED *against the* STRONG, "*so that the* SPOILED *shall come* AGAINST THE FOR- "TRESS. THEY HATE HIM THAT REBUKETH IN "THE GATE, AND THEY ABHOR HIM THAT "SPEAKETH UPRIGHTLY. *Forasmuch therefore*" (continues the Prophet) "*as your* TREADING IS UPON "THE POOR, *and ye take from him burthens of wheat,* "*ye have built houses of hewn stone, but ye shall not* "*dwell in them; ye have planted pleasant Vineyards,* "*but ye shall not drink wine of them. For I* KNOW "YOUR MANIFOLD TRANSGRESSIONS, *and your* "*mighty sins: they afflict the Just, they* TAKE A "BRIBE, *and they turn aside* THE POOR *in the Gate* "*from their right,*" &c. Amos v. 8 to 12.

" PRESSION and NATIONAL WICKED-
" NESS (163) *cannot escape a* NATIONAL
" PUNISHMENT, *according to the usual*
" *course of* GOD'S PROVIDENCE *in the*
" *World, unless a hearty Repentance and*
" *Amendment should avert the impending*
" *Vengeance.*"

(163) Extract of a letter from the Author to Lord ———, dated the 4th of December, 1774.

——————— ' If the seasonable warning against *the crying national wickedness of promoting the* AFRICAN SLAVE-TRADE, *and tolerating* SLAVERY *in Ameri-*
' ca, which I sent about three years ago, in a private
' letter to Lord ———, had been duly regarded, I sin-
' cerely believe that the present misunderstanding, &c.

* * * * * *

' and the alarming consequences which now threaten
' us, would not have happened!—*Great Britain and*
' *her Colonies* seem to be preparing themselves for
' MUTUAL * DESTRUCTION, which, alas! is too ap-
' parently merited on both sides: for such monstrous
' OPPRESSION and NATIONAL WICKEDNESS *cannot*
' *escape a* NATIONAL PUNISHMENT *according* to the
' usual course of God's providence in the World, un-
' less a hearty repentance and amendment should
' avert the impending vengeance!' &c.

* " For all the *Law is fulfilled in* ONE WORD (even) *in this*;
" *Thou shalt love thy Neighbour as thyself*. But if we bite and
" devour one another, take heed that YE BE NOT CONSUMED
" ONE OF ANOTHER." Gal. v. 14, 15. See my Tract on
" *The Law of Liberty, or Royal Law*."

This

This Doctrine is unqueſtionably demonſtrated (I truſt) by the ſeveral Extracts from the Holy Scriptures, which I have inſerted in the preceding pages: and the proof of it (I thank God) affords me a double recompence for my labours in collecting them; for it not only vindicates my previous aſſertions to the Miniſters of his preſent Majeſty, but it confirms the *ſimilar aſſertions* of my own Grandfather, declared, *near a Century ago*, to the great National Aſſembly of this Kingdom (164).

Can

---

(164) —— " Wicked men" (ſaid he) " may be
" happy and profperous here, and good men may
" ſuffer many afflictions and tribulations, without
" any the leaſt reflection on the juſtice or goodneſs of
" the great Governor of the World: becauſe there is
" a farther day reſerved for the adjuſting all men's
" rewards, according to their works. But now the
" conſideration of PUBLIC SOCIETIES and NATIONS
" is QUITE DIFFERENT. NATIONS *are not made to*
" *be* IMMORTAL, *but end with the world.* NO SOCI-
" ETY, AS A SOCIETY, SHALL BE CALLED TO A
" FUTURE ACCOUNT; *but all the rewards and pu-*
" *niſhments*

mies, whom God had delivered into their hands? And yet, we find, they were made mutual Instruments of Destruction to each other, on that very account!

Israel (I mean the Kingdom of the Ten Tribes) was the Scourge of *Judah*, *Judah* of *Israel*: *Syria* was the Scourge of both; as also were *Edom*, *Moab*, and *Ammon*: and *Assyria* was the Scourge of them all. *Egypt*, again, was the Scourge of *Assyria*; and *Assyria* (under a Babylonish King) became afterwards the severe Scourge and Retaliator of Evils upon *Egypt!*

The opulent *Tyre*, with her princely Merchants, suffered among the rest for her iniquitous Traffic in Slaves (165); and

(165) " *These enterprising Traders, the first great* " *Navigators of the World*" (says the sensible and benevolent Author of *Britannia Libera*), " *having, in* " *the*

and the lesser Philistine States, Ashdod, Gath, Gaza, &c. did not partake of the uncharitable *Crime*, without an equal share of *Retribution!*

These examples clearly demonstrate the necessity of observing the Apostle's Advice:—" *If ye bite and devour one* " *another, take heed that ye are not con-* " *sumed one of another*" (Gal. v. 15.): which is a striking representation of the EXTREME DANGER of *Oppression*

" *the course of their success and their grandeur, imported* " *for their own use a great number of* SLAVES, *they* " *conspired, slew their Masters, and all the Free-men*" (two only excepted, old STRATO and his Son, who were saved through the GENEROSITY OF THEIR OWN SLAVE) " *took to themselves their wives and daugh-* " *ters, with the whole city, and raised a new com-* " *monwealth;* A DREADFUL EXAMPLE, *faith Jus-* " *tin, to all the world,* * *who nevertheless went on in* " *their former course of* ENSLAVING *one another.*" Britannia Libera, or a Defence of the Free State of Man in England against the Claim of any Man there as a slave." p. 3.

* " CELEBRE HOC SERVORUM FACINUS, METUEN-" DUMQUE EXEMPLUM TOTO ORBE TERRARUM FUIT." Just. Hist. lib. xviii.

thers and Sisters ("*Men, Women, and Children*"), and then forcibly transporting them "*far from their border*," even to the opposite side (almost) of this terrestrial Globe!

What is this, my Countrymen, but a notorious aggravation of that very crime for which the *Vengeance* and *Retribution* of the ALMIGHTY was poured on the heads of the ancient Tyrian Merchants, above-mentioned. They

"*to try all the ways that are possible of making our peace with God, that so* INIQUITY MAY NOT BE OUR RUIN!" Archbp. Sharp's Sermons, Vol. 1. Serm. 8. p. 215, 216. 9th edit. But the horrible abomination of the Slave-Trade was only in its infancy when my Grandfather made this declaration, and the baneful tendency of it perhaps was hardly known to him, or he would certainly have entered a zealous and particular protest against it! With such an *accumulated load of national Guilt*, the necessity of a public humiliation and repentance is become more and more obvious, especially as the long foreseen *Vengeance of the Almighty* seems now ready to burst upon our heads! let us therefore earnestly join in the necessary reformation "*that so iniquity may not be our Ruin.*"

sold the Captive *Jews* to the Grecians, *a neighbouring People*; but YE HAVE SOLD the poor *Africans* (who never offended you) to *the very diſtant Inhabitants of America and the Weſt Indies*, "THAT "YE MIGHT REMOVE THEM FAR" (far indeed!) "FROM THEIR BOR-"DER." Have we not reaſon to expect the ſame awful Decree of the Divine Juſtice which immediately follows theſe words — "*Behold, I will raiſe them*" (i. e. the Slaves) "*out of the place* WHI-"THER YE HAVE SOLD THEM, *and* "*will return your Recompence upon your* "*own head*. AND I WILL SELL YOUR "SONS AND YOUR DAUGHTERS," &c. Joel iii. 7, 8. Have we not ample reaſon to fear, that God will make of this Nation (in proportion to the magnitude of our guilt in *Slave-dealing*) a tremendous Example of RETRIBUTION, to deter other Nations from offending his *Eternal* JUSTICE, if a ſincere and

ſpeedy

three years), warned the *House of Commons* concerning our *national Danger*.

But there is still one more great example against Tyranny and Oppression, which must not be omitted: I mean the example of God's Vengeance against Babylon, that great and terrible Scourge of all the other ancient Nations, already mentioned in this Tract; for as her OPPRESSIONS were more general and extensive, so her Punishment is more frequently and more fully declared in Scripture.

The Prophet Jeremiah denounced *the Law of Retribution* against the Babylonians in the strongest terms, as well in return for the cruel Slaughters they

'VENGEANCE OF THIS KIND.' Archbp. Sharp's Sermons, Vol. 2. Serm. 1. intitled, Repentance the Means for averting God's Judgement, 5th edit. p. 22. Preached before the House of Commons, April 11, 1679.

were

were guilty of, as for the heavy *Yoke of Bondage* with which they oppreſſed the Captive Iſraelites. See chap. L.—" *De-clare ye among the Nations*" (ſaid the Prophet), " *and publiſh, and ſet up a ſtandard; publiſh,* (and) *conceal not: ſay,* Babylon *is taken,* Bel *is confounded,*" &c. " For out of the North there cometh up a Nation againſt her, which ſhall" MAKE HER LAND DESOLATE ;" (manifeſtly in return for the cruel DESOLATION of Judea;) " *and none ſhall dwell therein*" (that is, in Babylon) : " *they ſhall remove, they ſhall depart, both Man and Beaſt.*" (Jer. L. 2, 3.) And to mark the *Indignation,* as well as *the Cauſe* of it, in the ſtrongeſt terms by the ſeverity of Contraſt, the Promiſe of a happy Reſtauration to the Captives, whom they oppreſſed, is blended with the Sentence of their own Condemnation :—" *In thoſe days, and at that time, ſaith the Lord, the Children*

" *of*

ample before quoted.) "*And I will* "BRING ISRAEL AGAIN TO HIS HA-"BITATION," &c.——"*Call together* "*the Archers against* BABYLON : *all* "*ye that bend the bow, camp against it* "*round about ; let none thereof escape :* "RECOMPENSE HER ACCORDING TO "HER WORK ; ACCORDING TO ALL "THAT SHE HATH DONE, DO UNTO "HER ; *for she hath been* PROUD *against* "*the Lord, against the Holy One of Israel.* "*Therefore shall her young men fall in the* "*streets.*" &c. And a little further the principal cause of God's Anger is more particularly expressed : — "*Thus saith* "*the Lord of Hosts ; The Children of* "*Israel and the Children of Judah* (were) "OPPRESSED TOGETHER : *and all that* "TOOK THEM CAPTIVES HELD THEM "FAST ; *they* REFUSED TO LET THEM "GO." But mark, ye *Slave-holders,* what immediately follows ! — "*Their* "REDEEMER *(is)* STRONG ; THE "LORD

"LORD OF HOSTS" (Jehovah of Armies) " (is) *his Name*; " *he shall* THOROUGHLY PLEAD THEIR CAUSE, *that he may give rest to the Land, and disquiet* THE INHABITANTS OF BABYLON —— A SWORD IS UPON THE CHALDEANS," &c. See the whole 50th chapter.

The *Law of Retribution* is also strongly marked in the 30th chapter, where the Prophet promises that Jehovah " *will* BRING AGAIN THE CAPTIVITY OF HIS PEOPLE ISRAEL AND JUDAH;" (ver. 2.) and *that* JACOB *shall be saved* OUT OF HIS TROUBLE, (ver. 7.) and more especially *from* SLAVERY, declaring, as the Word of the Lord of Hosts, " *I will break his* YOKE FROM OFF THY NECK, AND WILL BURST THY BONDS; *and* STRANGERS *shall no more* SERVE THEMSELVES OF HIM. *But they* SHALL SERVE THE LORD
" THEIR

" THEE *shall be* A SPOIL, *and all that*
" PREY UPON THEE *will I give* FOR A
" PREY: *for I will restore health unto*
" *thee, and I will heal thee of thy wounds,*
" *saith the Lord; because they called thee*
" AN OUTCAST (172), (saying,) *This*
" (is) *Zion, whom no man seeketh after.*"
&c.

In

(172) As it was manifestly an offence in the sight of God to call Israel an OUT-CAST *during the former* DESOLATION; it, certainly, *is not less so now*, tho' that devoted People is at present *dispersed over the face of all the Earth*, without a single Acre of *National* Territory in any one place! for the scriptures gives us ample assurance of a much more glorious *Return of the Jews*, than that from *Babylon*; and the Apostle to the Gentiles has expresly declared, that " *God hath* " *not* CAST AWAY *his people which he fore knew.*" Rom. xi. 2. And in the 11th verse he says, " *through* THEIR FALL *Salvation is come unto the* " *Gentiles for to provoke them to Jealousy. Now*" (says he) " *if the* FALL OF THEM *be the* RICHES OF THE " WORLD, *and* THE DIMINISHING *of* THEM *the* " RICHES OF THE GENTILES; HOW MUCH MORE " THEIR FULNESS?" &c. and again in the 15th verse—" IF THE CASTING AWAY *of them be the re-* " *conciling of the World, what shall the* RECEIVING " OF THEM BE, BUT LIFE FROM THE DEAD?"

And

In the 25th chapter also a severe *Retribution* is denounced expresly against
" *the*

And the apostle also warns us NOT *to boast against the Branches of that Mystical Olive Tree* on which the Wild Olive Tree of the Gentiles is grafted, "*for*" (says he) " *if God spared not the* NATURAL " BRANCHES" (the Israelites) *take heed lest he* ALSO " SPARE NOT THEE."—(and indeed we have the greatest reason to acknowledge the great mercy of God in sparing this nation hitherto, if we consider the many bloody persecutions of the Jews in this Kingdom during the dark days of POPISH IGNORANCE, (many particulars of which may be seen in Tovey's *Anglia Judaica*) or perhaps we may say, that many of the bloody Civil Wars and other *National Calamities*, that have already distressed *this Nation*, may have been inflicted on our ancestors for their *unmerciful Treatment* of these wandering STRANGERS in *persecuting, banishing, and even* MURDERING *them* in multitudes for the sake of plundering and robbing them of their wealth! Let us remember the confident hope of the Apostle, that the Israelites shall be again grafted into their own Olive Tree—"*for*" (says he) " *God is able to graff them in* " *again. For if thou wert cut out of the* OLIVE-TREE " *which is* WILD BY NATURE, *and wert* GRAFFED " *contrary to nature into a* GOOD OLIVE TREE; *how* " *much more shall these, which be* THE NATURAL " BRANCHES, *be* GRAFFED INTO THEIR OWN " OLIVE TREE?" and he adds, "*for I wou'd not,*
" *Brethren,*

after the return from the Babylonish Captivity;) *"and they shall cleave to "the House of* JACOB.*"* &c.——*"* And *"they shall take them* CAPTIVES WHOSE "CAPTIVES THEY WERE; *and they "shall rule over* THEIR OPPRESSORS." (This is a manifest RETRIBUTION IN KIND.) *"And it shall come to pass in " the day that the Lord shall give thee"* (Israel) *" rest from thy sorrow, and from " thy fear, and from the* HARD BON- "DAGE *wherein thou wast made to* "SERVE, *that thou shalt take up this " proverb against the* KING OF BABY- "LON, *and say, How hath* THE OP- "PRESSOR CEASED! *The Lord hath " broken the Staff of the Wicked,* (and) *" the Sceptre of the Rulers. He who "* SMOTE THE PEOPLE *in wrath with " a* CONTINUAL STROKE; *he that* " RULED THE NATIONS IN ANGER, *" is persecuted, and none hindereth."* &c. Isaiah xiv. 1—6. —— *" They that see " thee*

" *thee shall narrowly look upon thee,*
" (and) *consider thee,* (saying, is) *this*
" *the Man that made the Earth to trem-*
" *ble, that did shake Kingdoms?* (that)
" *made the World as a Wilderness, and*
" *destroyed the Cities thereof?* (that)
" OPENED NOT THE HOUSE OF HIS
" PRISONERS?" &c. Ver. 16, 17.
Mark this, ye hardened *Slave-holders,* who are so *tenacious* of that usurped and pretended property which ye claim in the Persons of your Fellow Men! Will ye also refuse to OPEN THE HOUSE OF YOUR PRISONERS? Remember that the same God still reigns, and never changes. If he spared not the first and most glorious Monarchy upon Earth, he surely will not spare you, unless ye sincerely repent and reform! God's Vengeance against Babylon was executed expressly on account of the *heavy Yoke of Bondage* with which they oppressed their Captives. The Judge-

poral and *spiritual*), proceeds to declare the reason of God's *severe Vengeance* against BABYLON in the 6th verse:—
"*I was wroth with my People, I have*
"*polluted mine Inheritance, and given them*
"*into* THINE HAND : *thou didst shew*
"*them* NO MERCY : *upon the Ancient*
"*hast thou* VERY HEAVILY LAID THY
"YOKE. *And thou saidst, I shall be a*
"*Lady for ever* : (so) *that thou didst*
"*not lay these* (things) *to thy heart,*
"*neither didst remember the latter end of*
"*it. Therefore hear now this, thou* (that
"art) *given to pleasures, that dwellest*
"*carelessly,*" &c.—" *These two things*
"*shall come to thee,* IN A MOMENT, IN
"ONE DAY ; *the loss of Children and*
"*Widowhood* ; *they shall come upon thee*
"*in their perfection, for the multitude of*
"*thy Sorceries,* (and) *for the great abun-*
"*dance of thine Enchantments. For thou*
"*hast trusted in thy Wickedness : thou hast*
"*said, None seeth me. Thy Wisdom and*
"*thy*

" *thy Knowledge it hath perverted thee.*" (Mark this, ye little Philosophers and sophistical Deists, who even make it a question whether there be such a thing as Providence in the World.) " *And* " *thou hast said in thine heart,* I (am), " *and none else beside me. Therefore shall* " *evil come upon thee ; thou shalt not know* " *from whence it riseth : and mischief* " *shall fall upon thee ; thou shalt not be* " *able to put it off : and* DESOLATION " *shall come upon thee* SUDDENLY (174), " (which)

(174) Compare this with the above-recited passage in the 9th verse : — " *These two things shall come to* " *thee,* IN A MOMENT, IN ONE DAY," &c. The same SUDDEN and UNEXPECTED VENGEANCE is also strongly described by Jeremiah : — " *Babylon*" (said he, in the spirit of Prophecy) " *is* SUDDENLY " FALLEN AND DESTROYED: HOWL FOR HER," &c. Chap. li. 8. This exemplary VENGEANCE was denounced expresly on account of the *Babylonian* TYRANNY *over the Jewish* CAPTIVES ; for in a preceding verse the latter are comforted, and informed of the RETRIBUTION determined against *Babylon :* — " *For Israel hath not been forsaken*" (said the Prophet) " *nor Judah, of his God, of the Lord of Hosts, though* " *their*

and the horrors of that fatal night were plainly foretold: — "*The night of my pleafure*"

"BABYLON *to deftroy it; becaufe it* (is) *the* VENGEANCE OF THE LORD, THE VENGEANCE OF HIS TEMPLE." Jer. li. 11. And in the 27th verfe the Prophet exprefsly names the Kingdoms from whence the feveral Armies that came with the MEDES and PERSIANS were raifed: — "*Set ye up a ftandard in the Land, blow the trumpet among the Nations, prepare the Nations againft her, call together againft her the Kingdoms of* ARARAT" *(viz.* in the neighbourhood of Armenia), "MINNI" (or Aram-Minni, the *Armenians* themfelves), "*and* ASHKENAZ" *(viz.* the Nations defcended from the eldeft Son of *Gomer*; who were nearly allied in blood to the *Medes, Madai* their Anceftor being a Brother of *Gomer*, as alfo of *Magog*, from whom the Turks have fince defcended, and all of them from the fame neighbourhood). "*Appoint a Captain againft her*" (who is afterwards declared to be CYRUS); "*caufe the* HORSES *to come up as the rough Caterpillars*" (the Perfians, as alfo the Parthians, and after them the Turks, likewife were ever famous for their Cavalry); "*prepare againft her the Nations, with the Kings of the* MEDES, *the Captains thereof, and all the Rulers thereof, and all the Land of his Dominion.*" &c. And in ver. 48 he fays, "*For the Spoilers* SHALL COME UNTO HER FROM THE NORTH." The Prophet Ifaiah alfo diftinctly pointed out the fame Inftruments of GOD's VENGEANCE againft *Babylon*: — "*Lift ye up the Banner*

"*upon*

"*pleasure*" (says the Prophet, manifestly referring to the impious midnight carousal

"*upon* THE HIGH MOUNTAIN; *exalt the voice unto* "*them*:" *&c.* describing the first mustering of the confederate Nations against the overgrown tyrannical power of *Babylon* :—" *The noise of a multitude* IN THE "MOUNTAINS" (probably meaning the Mountains of Ararat, *&c.* mentioned by Jeremiah) " *like as of a* "*great People; a tumultuous noise of the Kingdoms of* "*Nations gathered together:* THE LORD OF HOSTS" *(viz.* Jehovah of Armies) " *mustereth the Host of the* "*Battle.*" (Here we see the proper meaning of the Lord of Hosts.) " *They come from a far Country, from* "*the end of Heaven,* (even) *the Lord and the Weapons* "*of his indignation, to destroy the whole land, &c. Be-* "*hold I will stir up the* MEDES *against them, which* "*shall not regard Silver; and* (as for) *Gold they shall* "*not delight in it.* (Their) *Bows also*" (for the Medes were eminent Archers) " *shall dash the young* "*men to pieces: and they shall have no pity on the* "*fruit of the womb; their Eye shall not spare the Chil-* "*dren. And* BABYLON *the Glory of Kingdoms, the* "*beauty of the Chaldees excellency shall be as when God* "*overthrew Sodom and Gomorrah.*" &c. Chap. xiii. 2—19. Again in 21st chapter the same Prophet distinctly names the *Medes* and *Persians* to be the instruments of *God's* retribution against BABYLON. " *A* "*grievous Vision is declared unto me. The Treacherous* "*Dealer dealeth treacherously, and the Spoiler spoileth.* "*Go up,* O ELAM!" (for the *Persians* were descended

The Prophet Jeremiah alſo alludes to the ſame fatal Babylonian ſupper, which ſeems to have been intended as a *Feſtivity* to the honour of their Falſe Deities (179), in order to inſure ſucceſs againſt the Beſiegers:—" *In their* "*heat*" (or in their anger, that is, againſt their Enemies in the War) "*I will* " *make their* FEASTS, *and I will make* " *them* DRUNKEN, *that they may rejoice,* " *and ſleep a perpetual ſleep, and not* " *wake, ſaith the Lord. I will bring*

that *fatal night*, they found the King and his Princes aſſembled, and the King ſtanding with a drawn ſcymitar in his hand, ready to oppoſe them (notwithſtanding his extreme conſternation juſt before, on hearing the miraculous prediction of his fate), that he might endeavour to perſuade his *Princes* to ſtand by him, and reſiſt the Enemy; though, indeed, the learned Vitringa ſuppoſes. that the words " *ariſe,* " *ye Princes, and anoint the ſhield*" refer to the Speech of Cyrus juſt before the aſſault, recorded likewiſe by Xenophon—Αλλ' αγετε, λαμβανετε οπλα, *&c.*

(179) We read in Daniel v. 4. that " *they* DRANK " WINE, *and* PRAISED THE GODS OF GOLD, *and* " OF SILVER, *of braſs, of iron, of wood, and of ſtone.*"

" *them*

"*them down* LIKE LAMBS *to the slaugh-ter*" (that is, without opposition or resistance on their part (180), "*like Rams with He-goats. How is Sheshach taken! and how is the praise of the whole Earth surprized!*" (alluding to the unexpected entry of the Enemy;) "*How is Babylon become an astonishment among the Nations!*" &c. Jer. li. to ver. 42. And the *manner of bringing about* this VENGEANCE, as well as the REASON of it, is further described in the same chapter: —"*For the Lord God of* RECOMPENCES" (said the Prophet, ver. 56.) "*shall surely* REQUITE. *And I will*

---

(180) Which is described also in the 40th verse of the same chapter:—"*The mighty men of Babylon have forborne to fight, they have remained in their holds*; THEIR MIGHT HATH FAILED, *they* BECAME AS WOMEN: *they*" (that is, the Enemy) "*have burned her dwelling places; her bars are broken. One post shall run to meet another*, TO SHEW THE KING OF BABYLON *that his City is taken at one end, and that the passages are stopped, and the reeds they have burned with* FIRE, *and the men of war are affrighted.*" &c.

"MAKE

" *and glorified himself in Israel. Thus*
" *saith the Lord* THY REDEEMER, *and*
" *he that formed thee from the Womb;*
" *I* (am) *the* LORD" (Jehovah), " *that*
" *maketh all* (things) ; *that stretcheth*
" *forth the Heavens alone ; that spreadeth*
" *abroad the Earth by myself: that frus-*
" *trateth the Tokens of the Lyars, and*
" *maketh Diviners mad; that turneth*
" *Wise* (Men) *backward, and maketh*
" *their Knowledge foolish;*" (referring, probably, to the unprofitable Sciences and vain Politics of the Chaldeans ;)
" *that confirmeth the Word of his Servant,*
" *and performeth the Counsel of his Mes-*

Redeemer! " If the fall of them" (said the Apostle Paul) " be the *riches of the world,* and the diminish-
" ing of them the Riches of the Gentiles ; *how much*
" *more their fulness?*" Romans xi. 12. and he tells us again in the 25th verse, " *That Blindness in part is*
" *happened to Israel until the fulness of the Gentiles be*
" *come in, and so shall* ALL ISRAEL *be saved;*" &c. and again in the 32d verse—that " *God hath included them*
" ALL IN UNBELIEF *that he might have mercy upon*
" ALL."

" *sengers;*

"*sengers; that saith to* JERUSALEM, "THOU SHALT BE INHABITED" (that is, after the appointed *Desolation*), "*and to the Cities of* JUDAH, *Ye* "*shall be built, and I will raise up the* "*decayed places thereof: that saith to the* "*Deep*" (whereby, according to the Targum, BABEL is meant), "*Be* DRY, "*and I will* DRY UP *thy Rivers:*" (most probably alluding to the successful stratagem of Cyrus to *dry up the Rivers* by altering their Course, whereby he gained an unsuspected passage into the City through the emptied Channels (183): "*that saith of* CYRUS, "(he

---

(183) "In the language of the Prophets" (says Mr. Cruden in his Concordance) "*Waters* often denote a great multitude of *people*;"—and this prophecy perhaps might allude to the vast *conflux* of people at Babylon; that God would *dry them* up by making the place desolate; but yet the literal sense is certainly to be preferred, because it seems to have had a literal accomplishment in the successful stratagem of Cyrus abovementioned.——" Certè de Babylone est "sermo," (says the learned Forerius) "per quam "fluebant

"BY THY NAME, (am) *the God of Is-*
"*rael.*" And in the next verse the
Prophet assigns the reason why the Almighty thus called upon CYRUS, viz:
—" *for Jacob my Servant's sake, and Is-*
" *rael mine elect, I have even called thee*
" BY THY NAME: *I have* SURNAMED
" THEE, *though thou hast not known me.*
" *I* (am) *the Lord,*" (or rather *I* (am)
JEHOVAH) " *and* (there is) *none else,*
" (there is) *no God beside me: I girded*
" *thee,*" (or strengthened thee) " *though*
" *thou hast not known me,*" &c. and God's
PURPOSE in raising up CYRUS is still
more clearly declared in the 13th verse,
—" *I have raised him up in* RIGHTE-
" OUSNESS, *and I will* DIRECT ALL
" HIS WAYS: *he shall* BUILD MY CITY,
" *and* HE SHALL LET GO MY CAP-
" TIVES," (mark this ye wretched
Slave-holders) " NOT FOR PRICE, NOR
" REWARD, *saith the Lord of Hosts;*"
and accordingly *the Proclamation of Free-*
dom

dom to the Jews and the Decree for rebuilding the Temple were made in the first year of Cyrus. See Ezra i. 1.

Now let my Readers seriously compare these accounts of God's peculiar favour to CYRUS, THE RESTORER OF LIBERTY, with the accounts (which I have already recited) of GOD's opposite treatment of that man who " OPEN-
" ED NOT THE HOUSE OF HIS PRI-
" SONERS." Isaiah xiv. 17.

Cyrus by the Almighty was expressly called, in the 45th chapter of Isaiah, " HIS ANOINTED :"—" *Thus saith the* " *Lord to* HIS ANOINTED, *to* CYRUS ;" and למשיחו לכורש, literally " *to his* " *Messiah* (186), *to Cyrus,*" &c. for Cyrus

---

(185) In the Septuagint the passage is rendered τω Χρισω μυ Κυρω, and literally from thence in the Latin Vulgate " *Christo meo Cyro,*" to Cyrus my Christ.

many are they who, for the fake of a little worldly profit, are again entangled in the fnares and temptations of their *fpiritual Enemy*, and fubmit themfelves to his *Bondage!* How can we fuppofe, that thofe men are FREE from THE MAMMON OF UNRIGHTEOUSNESS, who are led by the temptations of pri-

ritance, (which they feemed to value above all other things) after fuffering the moft extraordinary flaughters and calamities of an unfuccefsful and deftructive war in defence of it, and of their TEMPORAL LIBERTIES! And they *remain in exile* to this day, a living Teftimony to the Truth of Prophecy*, and an Example to all the Nations, wherever they are difperfed, of GOD's VENGEANCE againft the Rejecters of his divine Revelation!

* " *And when he*" (Jefus) " *was come near*" (that is, to Jerufalem) " *he beheld the City, and* WEPT OVER IT, *faying,* " *If thou hadft known, even thou, at leaft in this thy day, the things* " (*which belong*) *unto thy peace! But now they are hid from thine* " *eyes. For the days fhall come upon thee that thine Enemies fhall* " *caft a Trench about thee, and compafs thee round, and keep thee in on* " *every fide,*" (and it is very remarkable, that the Romans, after trying all the ufual means in vain, fhould at length be obliged to have recourfe to *this method* before they could fucceed,) " *and* " *fhall lay thee even with the ground, and thy Children within thee:* " *and they fhall not leave in thee one ftone upon another, becaufe* " *thou knoweft not the time of thy vifitation.*" Luke xix. 41—44. Thus Chrift *proclaimed* "THE DAY OF VENGEANCE OF OUR " GOD,"—agreeable to Ifaiah's prophecy, already recited in this note, p. 299.

vate

vate interest to infringe the NATURAL RIGHTS OF MANKIND, by uncharitably retaining their *Fellow Men* in an *involuntary* SERVITUDE!

Can any injury, except that of *taking away a man's* LIFE, exceed that of *taking away a man's* LIBERTY, who has never offended us! Can any *robbery* or *injustice* whatsoever be more atrocious than that of wearing out our *poor Brethren* in a hard *involuntary service, without* WAGES *or* REWARD! thereby continually *robbing them of the Fruit of their Labours*! Have I not shewn, by unquestionable examples from Scripture, that this is *a crying sin,* and that the Almighty hath denounced Wo (187) against all such Offenders? Do we not

---

(187) " *Wo unto him that buildeth his House by Un-* " *righteousness, and his Chambers by Wrong;* (that) " USETH HIS NEIGHBOUR'S SERVICE WITHOUT " WAGES, AND GIVETH HIM NOT FOR HIS " WORK;" &c. Jer. xxii. 13.

profess

profess to serve THE SAME GOD who so severely punished the Jews for *this very crime?* And is there any just ground to hope, that GOD, who spared not his own peculiar People, will, nevertheless, excuse the Inhabitants of *Great Britain and her Colonies,* when they are *wilfully guilty* of the same offence!

The whole tenour of the Scriptures teaches us, that SLAVERY was ever *detestable in the sight of God,* insomuch that it has generally been denounced (and, of course, inflicted) as the punishment of the most abandoned Sinners; of which I have already given a great variety of instances.

Let us therefore, before it is too late, take warning by these tremendous examples of GOD's VENGEANCE against this kind of *Oppression,* which the Scriptures hold forth, not only to *this Nation*, but to all the World besides! The examples which I have quoted of *God's Vengeance*, denounced against the *Israelites* and *Jews* for TYRANNY, are not more striking than the examples of VENGEANCE denounced against the very *Instruments of that* VENGEANCE (the Assyrians and Babylonians) expressly on *the same account*; for though the latter were mere *Instruments in God's hand*, to punish the Jews *in kind*, yet they were themselves subjected to the like RETRIBUTION!

Nay, THE VENGEANCE was denounced particularly against the Chaldeans (and the cause of it, also, was declared) *long before they were guilty of the offence*, as I have before remarked, even while the Jews, the Nation vindicated by this punishment, were exercising that *Tyranny* at home for which they
were

were then doomed to the *Babylonian Yoke,* and thereby laid the foundation for the future retaliated CAPTIVITY *of their haughty* CONQUERORS *the Chaldeans!*

And have not we juſt reaſon to dread the ſevere VENGEANCE OF ALMIGHTY GOD, when it is notorious, that the *Tyranny* exerciſed in the Britiſh Colonies is infinitely more unmerciful than that which was formerly exerciſed by the *Chaldeans,* inſomuch that the ſtate of the Jews in their *Captivity* might be eſteemed rather as *Freedom* than *Bondage,* when compared with the *deplorable Servitude* of the wretched NEGRO SLAVES, as well as of the white Servants, in our Colonies?

What muſt be the conſequence of ſuch abominable wickedneſs?

By

By as much as we exceed the Assyrians and Babylonians in religious knowledge, by so much more severely may we expect the hand of God upon us for our monstrous abuse of such advantages!

The Inhabitants of *Great Britain* and the Inhabitants of *the Colonies* seem to be almost equally guilty of *Oppression!*

THE COLONIES *protest* against the Iniquity of the SLAVE-TRADE; but, nevertheless, continue to hold the poor wretched *Slaves* in a most *detestable Bondage!* GREAT BRITAIN, indeed, keeps *no Slaves*, but publicly encourages the *Slave-trade*, and contemptuously neglects or rejects every petition or attempt of the *Colonists* against that notorious wickedness!

The House of Burgesses in *Virginia*, transmitted a very sensible and respectful Petition to the King (188), dated the 1st of April, concerning the *Iniquity, Inhumanity,*

(188) Extracts from the minutes of the House of Burgesses in Virginia.

Wednesday, April 1st, 1772.

Most Gracious Sovereign,

WE your Majesty's dutiful and loyal subjects the Burgesses of Virginia, now met in general assembly, beg leave with all humility to approach your Royal Presence.

The many instances of your Majesty's benevolent intentions and most gracious disposition to promote the prosperity and happiness of your subjects in the colonies, encouraged us to look up to the Throne, and implore your Majesty's paternal assistance, in averting *a Calamity of a most alarming nature.*

The importation of slaves into the colonies from the coast of Africa hath long been considered as a trade of *great Inhumanity*, and under its present encouragement, we have too much reason to fear *will endanger the very existence of your Majesty's American dominions.*

We are sensible that some of your Majesty's subjects in Great Britain may reap emolument from this sort of Traffic; but when we consider that it greatly retards the settlement of the colonies with *more white inhabitants,* and may *in time have the most destructive influence,*

Inhumanity, and *destructive Influence* of the AFRICAN SLAVE-TRADE, to which

influence, we presume to hope, that the interest of a few will be disregarded, when placed in competition with the security and happiness of such numbers of your Majesty's dutiful and loyal subjects.

Deeply imprest with these sentiments, we most humbly beseech your Majesty to remove all those restraints on your Majesty's Governors of this colony, which inhibit their assenting to such laws as might check so very pernicious a commerce.

Your Majesty's antient colony and dominion of Virginia hath at all times, and upon every occasion, been entirely devoted to your Majesty's sacred person and government; and we cannot forego this opportunity of renewing those assurances of the truest loyalty and warmest affection, which we have so often, with the greatest sincerity, given to the best of Kings, whose wisdom and goodness we esteem the surest pledge of the happiness of all his people.

Resolved, nemine contradicente, That the House doth agree with the Committee in the said address to be presented to his Majesty.

Resolved, That an address be presented to his Excellency the Governor, to desire that he will be pleased to transmit the address to his Majesty, and to support it in such manner as he shall think most likely to promote the desirable end proposed.

(C O P Y.)

not the least Answer hath yet been returned!

The Freeholders and Inhabitants of the County of *Somerset*, in *New Jersey*, also, through their " *regard to the civil and* RELIGIOUS *Interest of the Country, and the established Rights of Mankind*," presented to the Governor, Council, and Representatives of that Province a very seasonable Testimony against that wicked " *Traffic which has Slavery for it's object*," praying them to " *provide against the future Importation of Slaves into that Colony*," and " *to enable such persons as shall chuse it to manumit their* SLAVES *upon equitable Principles to the Owners and the Public*," &c. (189).

---

(189) To the Governor, Council, and Representatives of the Province of New Jersey, in General Assembly met.

The Petition of sundry Freeholders and Inhabitants of the County of Somerset,

Respectfully

Another Petition upon the like benevolent principles was prefented to the fame Affembly by "*divers Inhabitants of the County of* Essex *in the faid Province,*" wherein they alfo fignified their diffatisfaction concerning "*an Act of Affembly in force for preventing the manu-*

Refpectfully fheweth,

THAT your Petitioners, influenced with an equal regard to the civil and religious interefts of this Province and the eftablifhed Rights of Mankind, have with concern often viewed that Traffic, which has *Slavery* for it's object, in a light very *unfriendly* to both; and it has afforded pleafure to obferve the liberal advances which of late have been made among all ranks of people towards the difcountenance of that Trade, and promotion of Juftice to thofe who have thereby been deprived of their *Liberty*. Hence your Petitioners are induced to addrefs the Legiflature, and to requeft, that a fubject fo important may receive that attention which it deferves. Your Petitioners alfo beg, that you will not only provide againft the future importation of Slaves into this Colony, by fuch ways as you may think beft, but to enable fuch perfons as fhall chufe it to manumit them by making them ufeful and happy upon equitable principles to the Owners and the Public, as in your wifdom may appear moft conducive to thofe good ends. And your Petitioners fhall pray, &c.

"*mitting*

against the African Trade in a pathetic and earnest Petition to their Provincial Assembly; wherein they take notice of the example set them by the Province of *Virginia* in petitioning the King, " *from a deep sensibility of the danger and* " *pernicious consequences which will be* " *attendant on a Continuation of this most* " *iniquitous Traffic*" (191). But the Assembly,

---

(191) To the Representatives of the Freemen of the Province of Pennsylvania in Assembly met.

The Petition of a number of the Inhabitants of the City and County of Philadelphia,

Respectfully sheweth,

THAT the importation of the natives of Guinea, to be sold and used as slaves in the provinces and islands of the British dominions in America, has long been an occasion of deep concern to a great number of the Inhabitants of this province, as well on account of its inconsistency with the whole tenor of the Christian religion, as because of the evil influence it has on the religious and moral conduct of the people, and the dreadful consequence which, it is to be feared, will one day attend in those parts where it prevails.

We

sembly, being desirous first to know what reception the abovementioned neglected *Virginian* Petition had met with at Court, postponed their address to the Throne; and instead of it transmitted

"We are the more encouraged to lay this important object before you, as we understand some of the colonies have been led into serious consideration, as well of the iniquity of the practice, as of the dangerous situation some of them are in, particularly the province of *Virginia*, whose House of Burgesses has lately *petitioned the King*, from a deep sensibility of the danger, and pernicious consequences which will be attendant on a continuation of this MOST INIQUITOUS TRAFFICK.

We your petitioners, therefore, most earnestly beseech you, to take this matter, which we apprehend to be of the utmost consequence to the welfare and safety of the British colonies, under your most serious consideration, and to use your utmost endeavours with the other colonies, in making such representations to the King as to you may appear most effectual towards putting a stop to this mighty evil."

Signed by about two hundred persons, amongst whom were, the provost of the academy, and three other clergymen of the church of England, being all that are in this city, five Presbyterian Clergymen, and four other Ministers, the rest respectable Inhabitants.

cation! Surely *he hath expected better things of us!* Have we not juſt reaſon to fear that he will condemn this nation as he did the Jews of old? ſaying—
" *he looked for* JUDGEMENT, *but behold*
" OPPRESSION; *for* RIGHTEOUSNESS,
" *but behold a* CRY!" Iſaiah v. 7.

As God never changes, it is impoſſible that this nation ſhould eſcape his *juſt retribution*, and ſtill perſiſt in violating *the natural Rights* of mankind!

Reflect, my Countrymen, for a moment, upon the preſent ſtate of thoſe enormous national Tranſgreſſions, the *African Slave Trade* encouraged *in* GREAT BRITAIN, and the *toleration of Slavery* in THE BRITISH COLONIES, and you will readily perceive that we muſt ſtand *condemned* even if we *judge ourſelves!* and how then ſhall we appear before that

that Righteous *Judge*, who is no respecter of persons? How can we hope to escape the DIVINE VENGEANCE when we know that the Almighty hath even *bound himself* with a most solemn oath never to forget *any such acts of* OPPRESSION ? " *The Lord hath sworn by the* " *excellency of Jacob,* SURELY *I will* " *never forget any of their works,*" or rather " *all their works,*" כל מעשיהם ; amongst which the SLAVE-TRADE, in particular, is expresfsly mentioned in the preceding verse, *viz.* " *buying the* " *Poor for Silver,*" &c. And then he condescends *to appeal,* as I before remarked, to *human Judgement* concerning the propriety, or rather the necessity and certainty, of the Divine Vengeance for such National Wickedness!—" *Shall not the Land tremble for* " *this? and every one mourn that dwelleth* " *therein?*" Amos viii. 6—8. And in
like

" green tree. *Wherefore the Lord his*
" *God delivered him into the hand of the*
" *King of* SYRIA; *and they smote him,*
" *and* CARRIED AWAY A GREAT
" MULTITUDE OF THEM CAPTIVES,
" *and brought* (them) *to* DAMASCUS.
" *And he was also delivered into the hand*
" *of the King of* ISRAEL, *who smote him*
" *with a great slaughter: for* PEKAH"
(the King of Israel) " *the Son of* RE-
" MALIAH *slew in Judah* AN HUNDRED
" AND TWENTY THOUSAND IN ONE
" DAY, *all valiant men;* BECAUSE THEY
" HAD FORSAKEN THE LORD GOD OF
" THEIR FATHERS. *And* ZICHRI, *a*
" *mighty man of Ephraim, slew* MAA-
" SEIAH THE KING'S SON, *and* AZ-
" RIKAM THE GOVERNOR OF THE
" HOUSE, *and* ELKANAH (that was)
" NEXT TO THE KING. *And the Chil-*
" *dren of* ISRAEL *carried away captive*
" *of their Brethren* TWO HUNDRED
" THOUSAND WOMEN, SONS AND
" DAUGH-

" DAUGHTERS, *and took also away much*
" *spoil from them, and brought the spoil*
" *to Samaria. — But a Prophet of the*
" *Lord was there whose name* (was)
" ODED: *and he went out before the*
" *Host that came to Samaria,*" (tha tis, as
they returned from the War to Samaria
with their Captives and Booty,) " *and*
" *said unto them,* " *Behold, because the*
" LORD GOD *of your Fathers was wroth*
" *with Judah, he hath delivered them*
" *into your hand, and ye have* SLAIN
" THEM IN A RAGE (that) REACH-
" ETH UP UNTO HEAVEN. *And now*"
(said the Prophet) " *ye purpose to* KEEP
" UNDER *the Children of Judah and Je-*
" *rusalem for* BOND-MEN *and* BOND-
" WOMEN *unto you:* (but are there)
" NOT WITH YOU, EVEN WITH YOU,
" SINS *against the* LORD *your* GOD?
" *Now hear me therefore, and* DELIVER
" THE CAPTIVES AGAIN, *which ye*
" *have* TAKEN CAPTIVE OF YOUR
" BRETHREN:

This reason, as well as the undaunted Resolution of those who gave it, had the proper effect upon the Israelitish Soldiers, who, notwithstanding the general depravity of their countrymen, *still deserved the name of* MEN, by demonstrating, that they were not insensible to REASON, and that they thought themselves entitled (though SOLDIERS) to that *common Right of* HUMAN NATURE, *the Right of judging for themselves in matters of conscience,* without which no man can be truely *honourable:* for as soon as they heard the just remonstrance of the four Noblemen, they quitted *the Prey* and *the Plunder* (a hard thing for Soldiers to submit to) without waiting, it seems, for the word of command from the King or his Princes! —" *So the armed men*" (says the Text) " *left the Captives and the Spoil before* " THE PRINCES *and* ALL THE CONGREGATION." Ver. 14.

Here

[325]

Here (be pleased to observe) is a *National Council* at once assembled in the field; *the whole Power of the People—* " THE PRINCES AND ALL THE CON-
" GREGATION."

What were their Deliberations on this occasion does not appear, nor their RESOLUTIONS, or rather, they seem to have been totally IRRESOLUTE, wavering between what was a RIGHT TO BE DONE and PRIVATE INTEREST; as if each man was unwilling to give up his *share of the booty*, and yet ashamed openly to resist the active Resolution of the four Chiefs on so charitable a cause; for these four Noblemen, it seems, at last boldly took upon themselves the whole business;—" *and the men*" (says the Text) " *which were expressed by name*," (viz. the four Noblemen mentioned in the 12th verse) " ROSE UP, *and* TOOK
" THE CAPTIVES, *and* WITH THE
" SPOIL

they have not the leaft pretence of war or quarrel)——" MEN AND WOMEN, " SONS AND DAUGHTERS"——" FOR " BONDMEN AND FOR BONDWOMEN" to be worn out with unremitted labour, like thofe poor injured creatures whofe places they fupplied!—*Great Britain*, I fay, with all this accumulated load of guilt has not yet produced *four Chiefs or Noblemen* to PROTEST againft this moft abominable Tyranny, and " to " *ftand in the Gap*," with reverential fear of God, to avert the DIVINE VENGEANCE, though *Religion*, *Humanity*, and even *Common Senfe* ought to have prompted them to it!—May we not too aptly compare the principal crimes of the *Jews*, (for which *they loft their liberty*), to the prefent crying Sins of GREAT BRITAIN AND HER COLONIES! —" *In the midft of thee*" (faid a Prophet from God) " *have they* DEALT " BY OPPRESSION WITH THE STRAN- " GER:

" GER : *in thee have they vexed the
" Fatherless and the Widow.*" Ezek.
xxii. 7. And again, " *The People of
" the Land have used* OPPRESSION *and
" exercised* ROBBERY, *and have vexed
" the Poor and Needy: yea, they have
"* OPPRESSED THE STRANGER WRONG-
" FULLY. *And I sought for* A MAN
" *among them that should make up the
" hedge, and* STAND IN THE GAP *be-
" fore me for the Land, that I should not
" destroy it: but I found none!* THERE-
" FORE *have I poured out mine indigna-
" tion upon them, I have consumed them
" with the fire of my wrath:* THEIR
" OWN WAY *have I* RECOMPENSED
" UPON THEIR HEADS, *saith the Lord
" God.*" Ezek. xxii. 29—31. And have
not the Inhabitants of *Great Britain* and
her *Colonies,* therefore, just reason to expect a *similar* VENGEANCE for *the like* OP-
PRESSIONS ? Do they flatter themselves,
that the *same God* will permit them to go

your Order, in particular, with the omiſſion. The *crying Sin* has hitherto been

ſincere perſonal reſpect and eſteem for ſeveral truly worthy and learned Individuals of that order, now living, but I am even deſcended from one of the ſame holy function, who in his correſpondence with foreign Proteſtant churches, very ably defended and promoted the *Eſtabliſhment of Epiſcopacy*; and, above all, I am thoroughly convinced by the Holy Scriptures that the inſtitution of THAT ORDER in the Chriſtian Church IS OF GOD; and that the only defect in the *Engliſh Eſtabliſhment* of it, is the want of a FREE ELECTION * to the Office. For as it may clearly be proved

---

* The learned Judge Blackſtone, in his Commentaries, book I. c. 11. p. 377. informs us, that "ELECTION *was, in* VERY "EARLY TIMES, *the uſual mode of Elevation to the* EPISCO- "PAL CHAIR *throughout all Chriſtendom; and this*" (ſays he) "*was promiſcuouſly performed by the* LAITY, *as well as by the* "CLERGY," ("*per* CLERUM *&* POPULUM :") for which he cites very ample authorities. But afterwards a complaint of *tumultuous Elections*, together with the ſuppoſed Royal Prerogative of granting the Inveſtiture of *Temporalities* (though the *Temporalities*, being originally granted to ſupport the *Dignity* of the Office, cannot reaſonably be ſo far drawn from the firſt intention, as to deprive the Office of that real *Dignity* which ariſes from a free Election) ſerved the deſigns of Emperors and Kings as *a pretence* to invade *the Freedom of Election*; and the ſame *pretence* of TUMULT proved equally favourable to the oppoſite deſigns of Popes; ſo that theſe jarring intereſts ſeemed united, however, in their endeavours (as it were by one Spirit of *Antichriſt)* to deprive the Church of her *ancient Right*, which

(had

been far distant from your *sight*, and perhaps was never fully represented to you,

proved that the *Churches of Britain and Ireland* have a just and ancient *Right* to *elect* their own Bishops, and did actually exercise that right for many ages, till the antichristian Usurpations of *Monks* and *Popes* over the secular

(had it been maintained) would probably have prevented most of the future usurpations of the *Papal Antichrist*; and therefore " *the Policy of the Court of Rome at the same time began by de-* " *grees to* EXCLUDE THE LAITY *from any share in these* " ELECTIONS," (says the learned Judge Blackstone,) " *and* " *to confine them wholly to the* CLERGY, *which at length was* " *completely effected.*" 1 Blackstone, c. 11. p. 378. The original ground for the complaint of *tumult* in these *Elections* was probably occasioned by the neglect of that unexceptionable Apostolic mode of Election described in Acts i. 15 to 26; for when Christianity began to be corrupted by Vows of *Celibacy*, and other Popish and Diabolical Doctrines, the *Clergy* and *Laity* began to have opposite interests to serve (which ought never to be) in the Choice of their Bishop, and, of course, the two contending parties would reciprocally depend upon their own activity, zeal, or address for success in the *Election*; so that *Tumult* (the old complaint) must be the necessary consequence; whereas had it been an indispensible form to nominate TWO qualified persons (viz. either *two* by the promiscuous suffrages of both parties, or *one* by each party), and afterwards, *in solemn prayer*, to submit the final decision to the Providence of God by a Lot (as in the *Apostolic Election*), there could be no room for contention: the undue influence and partiality of *Individuals* would be effectually checked; and, above all, the joint prayers of *both parties*, in an appeal to God's decision, would certainly add *Solemnity* (instead of *Tumult*) to the *Election*, if not also much additional

for affiftance! *Ye know the Scriptures,* and therefore to you, my Lords, in particular

perverfion of that juft and ancient *Right* † abovementioned, and is entirely deftructive of all the defirable purpofes of a free *Election.* This practice, however, cannot be cenfured in ftronger terms than thofe in which

pointment of *two* perfons by the *Congregation* or 'Οχλος :—" *Hæc* " *oratio*" (fays he, fpeaking of Peter's Addrefs to the People) " *quum placuiffet* MULTITUDINI *ftatuerunt* DUOS," *&c.* And a little afterwards he gives the following commendation of that primitive example :—" *Tametfi* SORTES *periculofæ non funt, quæ* " *utriucunque faverint, probum & idoneum defignant. Nec totum* " *negotium creditum eft* SORTIBUS. SUFFRAGIIS *funt electi* " DUO *probatiffimi. Inter hos ambiguitatem Electionis finiit* SORS, " *quæ nec ipfa temeritatem habere potuit, cujus eventum moderatur* " *precatio.* SORS *igitur hæc, quæ nihil aliud fuit quàm* DECLA- " RATIO DIVINÆ VOLUNTATIS, *defignavit* MATTHIAM, " *quanquam* JOSEPH *præter cognominis*" (viz. Juftus) " *com-* " *mendationem, etiam* JESU *propinquitate commendebatur. Et* " *tamen huic prælatus eft Matthias, quo nos doceremur* IN DELI- " GENDIS EPISCOPIS, *quibus credenda fit Evangelicæ Doctrinæ* " *difpenfatio, adeo nihil effe tribuendum humanis affectibus*," *&c.*

† In a little Tract (by *John Barnes,* an Englifh Benedictine) intituled, *Sententia de Ecclefiæ Britannicæ Privilegiis,* which was printed together with fome little Tracts of Archbifhop Ufher in 1687, we find ftill a more ample teftimony of the *ancient Right* of chufing *Bifhops* :—" *Cùm* ANTIQUI MORES *Ecclefiæ* " *fuæ*" (fpeaking of the ancient BRITISH, SCOTCH, and IRISH) " *poftularent ut* OMNIA *inter fe* SYNODICE *agerent,* " *tum pro* EPISCOPORUM ORDINATIONIBUS, *tum pro aliis* " *negotiis Ecclefiafticis. Verba eorum ex* BEDA, *lib.* ii. *c.* 2. *Ec-* *clef. Hift. funt,* QUOD NON POSSUNT ABSQUE SUORUM CON-
SENSU

particular I appeal! If I have misrepresented *the Word of God,* on which my *Opposition*

which it is expressly condemned by a *subsequent Act of Parliament,* (1 Edw. VI. chap. ii.) though the former Act is supposed to be still in force, viz. " *The said* " ELECTIONS *be in very deed* NO ELECTIONS *but only* " *by*

SENSU ET LICENTIA PRISCIS ABDICARE MORIBUS." P. 154. And after citing an example from *Bede,* concerning *the Election of a Bishop* (viz. Aidan) by a Scotch Synod, at the request of the Saxon King *Oswald,* to instruct and preside over the Ministry of the newly converted Saxon or English Church (see p. 154 and 155), he further remarks :—" *Et ex* HUNTING" DONIENSI" (says he) " *lib.* iii. *Hist. &* BED. *lib.* ii. *constat* " ET SCOTOS ET BRITANNOS OMNIA SUA COMMUNI CON" SENSU EGISSE."

It appears also, that the *Saxon* or *English* Church, though much less ancient than the *British, Irish,* and *Scotch* Churches, did yet enjoy the same inestimable privilege of *electing Bishops.* The Monk *Matthew Paris* has transmitted to us a memorable example of this, in his Account of the Election, A. D. 1095, of the celebrated *Ulstan* to be Bishop of Worcester :—" *Processu au-* " *temtemporis* ULSTANUS (ELECTO *ad Archiepiscopatum Ebora-* " *censem* ALDREDO) *unanimi consensu, tam* CLERI *quam* TO" TIUS PLEBIS, *Rege insuper ut quem vellent sibi eligerent prae-* " *sulem & animarum Pastorem annuente,* IN EPISCOPUM *ejus-* " *dem loci* ELIGITUR." P. 20. And even in later times, when *the Romish Corruptions* had so far prevailed as to exclude the LAITY from Elections, yet the Clergy still enjoyed " *the free* " *right of electing their Prelates, whether Abbots or Bishops;*" for the learned Judge Blackstone informs us, that *this right* was granted in a charter " *to all the Monasteries and Cathedrals in the* " *Kingdom*" by King John, see vol. i. p. 379; and also that " *this grant was expressly recognized and confirmed in King John's* " MAGNA

Opposition to SLAVERY is founded, point out my errors, and I submit: but if, on the other hand, you should perceive that the Texts here quoted are really appli-

" *by a Writ of* CONGE D'ESLIRE, *have colours, sha-*
" *dows, and pretences of Elections, serving nevertheless*
" *to no purpose,*" &c.

If it had not been for this notorious defect in point of *Election*, and the general idea of its *consequences*, I am

" MAGNA CARTA, *and was again established by* STATUTE
" 25 *Edward* III. *St.* 6. § 3." *Ibid.* This Statute first gave *parliamentary authority*, indeed, to the King's *Congé D'Eslire* (though it was in use long before), and acknowledges the King's Right of *Assent* or Approbation " *after the Election*;" yet it contains nothing which can remove the prudent and reasonable limitation to which that *Assent* or *Approbation* was formerly subject, viz. that it " WAS NOT TO BE DENIED WITHOUT A
" REASONABLE AND LAWFUL CAUSE." Judge Blackstone, b. i. c. 11. p. 379. And this very Act (which was manifestly ordained to restrain the simoniacal practices and shameful usurpations of the Bishops of Rome) expressly acknowledges the Right of FREE ELECTIONS in the Church, viz. " that the FREE
" ELECTIONS of the Archbishops, Bishops, and all other Digni-
" ties and Benefices ELECTIVE *in England*, shall hold," &c. The *Right* was also fully established by preceding Statutes, still *in force*, though (unhappily for this Kingdom) not *in use*; as —" There shall be FREE ELECTION *of Dignities of the Church.*" 9 *Edward* II. c. 14. Title. And again, " ELECTIONS OUGHT
" TO BE FREE." 3 *Edward* I. c. 5. Mr. Ruffhead, in his useful Index to the Statutes, very properly refers us, under the head of " ELECTION OF BISHOPS," to this last-mentioned Statute;

applicable to the question before us, that my conclusions from thence are fairly drawn, and that the Examples of GOD's VENGEANCE against TYRANTS and SLAVE-HOLDERS ought strictly to warn us against *similar Oppressions* and *similar Vengeance*, you will not then, I trust, be backward *in this Cause of* GOD *and* MAN. *Stand up* (let me intreat you) "*for the Land;* MAKE UP THE "HEDGE," to save your Country; perhaps it is not yet too late! Enter a solemn protest, my Lords, against those who "*have oppressed the Stranger wrong-* "*fully.*" Ye know that the Testimonies I have quoted are of God! Warn

am persuaded that the late worthy Primate of England, would not have found such opposition in his endeavours some few years ago to promote *the establishment of* EPISCOPACY *in America!*

Statute; for *Episcopal Elections* ought certainly to be included in the meaning of the said Statute, as well as *all other Elections*; for an ELECTION without a CHOICE is a manifest contradiction in terms, and NO ELECTION.

there-

therefore the Nobles and Senators of these Kingdoms, that they incur not a double load of Guilt! as the burthen, not only of the *much-injured African Strangers*, but also of *our Country's Ruin*, must rest on the heads of those who withhold their Testimony against the CRYING SIN of TOLERATED SLAVERY! For " I KNOW *that the* LORD *will main-*
" *tain the* CAUSE *of the Afflicted, and*
" *the* RIGHT *of the Poor*." Psa. cxl. 12.

        GRANVILLE SHARP.

SOLI DEO GLORIA ET GRATIA.

TEXTS OF SCRIPTURE
QUOTED OR ILLUSTRATED
IN THE FOREGOING TRACT.

Genesis.

Chapter.	Verse.	Page.
XV.	11.	182
XVII.	8.	81

Exodus.

II.	23, 24.	12
III.	7, 8.	13
XXI.	2, 5, 6.	4, 5, 81, 173
XXII.	21—24.	16
XXIII.	9.	15

Leviticus.

XIX.	18, 33, 34.	10, 11
XXV.	10, 39, 40.	4, 173

Deuteronomy.

V.	15.	14
VII.	2, 16.	8, 9
X.	17—19.	10
XV.	12, 15.	173, 178, 195
XVI.	12.	178, 195
XXIII.	15, 16.	21
XXIV.	18, 22.	178—195

Judges.

VI.	8.	14

I Samuel.

Chapter.	Verse.	Page.
VII.	5—7	199
XXI.	1, 2, 3—9, 11, 12.	29, 30, 36, 142
XXII.	{ 1—3, 5—9, 13, 18, 19, 24—28, 30. }	97, 103, 137, 142, 301.
XXIII.	1, 2, 5, 6.	112, 162
XXIV.	1, 5, 7—9.	114, 138, 169
XXV.	1—9, 11—14.	81, 82, 124, 275
XXVI.	1—15.	76, 77
XXVII.	4—7.	85, 209.
XXX.	2, 7—9, 11, 16.	269—272.
XXXIII.	15, 16.	163
XXXIV.	1—3, 11.	28, 176
XXXV.	11.	88
XXXVI.	1—3, 5, 9, 29, 30.	85, 89, 94, 95, 97
XXXVII.	4—17.	185—187
XXXVIII.	2—5, 9—13.	189, 190
XXXIX.	1—7, 10.	27, 136, 137, 201, 206
XLV.	1, 5.	87
XLIX.	34, 39.	116, 117
L.	2—15, 33, 41—43.	148, 265—269, 287
LI.	1—42, 59—64.	119, 287—290
LII.	9—11, 31—34.	27, 48, 139, 203

LAMENTATIONS.

IV.	5, 9, 10.	200, 201
V.	13.	205

EZEKIEL.

VII.	3, 4, 8, 9, 11, 23.	31
XII.	19.	32
XVII.	15—21.	120—123
XXII.	7.	33, 34
XXIX.	3, 4.	122
XXXIX.	10.	262

DANIEL.

I.	1—3.	79, 90, 134
V.	4, 6.	286, 288

HOSEA.

V.	8.	75

JOEL.

JOEL.

Chapter	Verse	Page
III.	7, 8.	227, 261

AMOS.

Chapter.	Verse.	Page.
I.	1—15.	230—242
II.	1—6.	242, 246
III.	9—11.	246—250
V.	7—12.	247—249
VIII.	4—8.	23

OBADIAH.

I.	9—15.	227—229

MICAH.

III.	11.	69

ZECHARIAH.

VII.	3, 5.	89
VIII.	19.	Ibid.

MATTHEW.

I.	12.	135
VI.	24, 33.	113, 143
VII.	7.	197

MARK.

XI.	24.	197.

LUKE.

IV.	17—21.	299
X.	18.	196
XI.	9, 13.	197
XVI.	13.	197—143

JOHN.

I.	12.	196
X.	11.	163
VIII.	34.	145
XIV.	13.	197
XV.	7.	197

ROMANS.

[348]

Retribution denounced by him againſt the Syrians for their oppreſſions, 229. Againſt the Philiſtines, 231. Againſt Tyre, 235. Againſt Edom, 237. Againſt the bloody-minded Ammonites, 240. Againſt Moab, 242. Againſt Judah, 245. And, laſtly, againſt Iſrael, 246.

Armies, ſtanding, a warning example againſt the keeping of, 56, *note*.

Aſſyrians and Babylonians, inſtruments in the hand of God for the mutual puniſhment of each other, 210. Remarkable inſtance of divine vengeance againſt the former, 216, *note*.

B.

Babylon, the Prophet Jeremiah's denunciation of retribution againſt, 264. A prior denunciation againſt, by Iſaiah, 275. The bondage with which her captives were oppreſſed, the cauſe of God's vengeance againſt, 277. The ſtratagem by which Cyrus entered the City, 293. Great treaſures found in the chapels of the idols, 295.

Barnes, his account of the ancient mode of chooſing Biſhops, 334, *note*.

Bengelius, his account of the primitive mode of electing Biſhops, 334, *note*.

Biſhops, appeal to, and call upon them to exert their influence againſt negro-ſlavery, 331. The order of, a divine inſtitution, 332, *note*. Defect in the Engliſh eſtabliſhment of, *ibid*. The preſent mode of electing, a total perverſion of the primitive one, 334, *note*. This preſent mode expreſsly condemned by Act of Parliament, 337, *note*.

Blackſtone,

Blackstone, Judge, his account of the ancient mode of electing Bishops, 332, *note*. This right how usurped from the Laity, 333, *note*.

Britain; warnings to the inhabitants of, for tolerating, by *National Authority*, the oppression of African *Strangers* in the Colonies, 16, 34. Indications of the Devil's empire over, 146, *note*. Unjust laws pointed out, 213, *note*. Symptoms of national destruction, 226, *note*. Inquiry whether the corruptions and injustice which have destroyed other nations, may not draw down God's vengeance on them, 248, *note*. Cannot expect to be the only exception to God's general rule of national retribution, 258, 302.

C.

Christian Dispensation, Charity and Benevolence duties of indispensable obligation under, 6. Will not justify holding men in slavish bondage, *ibid*.

Churches of Britain and Ireland, how deprived of the just and ancient right of electing their own Bishops, 333, *note*.

Colonies, British, the oppressive treatment of negroes in, far exceeding those practices for which the Jews were reproached by their Prophets, 25. Number of negro slaves annually purchased there, 147. More tyranny exercised over the negroes there than formerly by the Chaldeans over the Jews, 304. And have reason therefore to expect more severe punishment, 305. Protest against the slave trade, yet at the same time continue to hold slaves in bondage, *ibid*.

Y y   Covetousness,

chadnezzar, 89. Is taken a second time, 99. Is taken a third time, 106.

Jewish servitude, the nature of under the Mosaic law, explained, 4.

Jews, the permission granted them of keeping bondsmen, cannot be claimed by any other nation, 8. The strongest instances of God's vengeance against tyrants, to be found in their history, 11. Their restoration to *natural freedom* from Egyptian *slavery*, the first *national mercy* they experienced, 12. This deliverance frequently mentioned by the prophets, 13. And particularly recommended to their remembrance, 14. That they might be moved to sympathize with *oppressed* strangers, 15. Warnings given them of the danger of *oppression*, 16. Their *oppressions* trivial in comparison with the treatment of negroes in the British Colonies, 25. The judgements of God executed against king Zedekiah, his family, and the nobles of Judah, 202. Under their present dispersion, have scriptural assurances of a glorious re-establishment, 272, *note*. Their final conversion will be a true object of general joy, 291, *note*.

Josephus, his disingenuous attempt to conceal the taking of Jerusalem by Nebuchadnezzar, 89, *note*. His account of the death of Jehoiakim, 98.

Josiah king of Judah, account of his sons, 44. The judgement he drew on himself by undertaking an unjust war against Pharaoh Necho, king of Egypt, 155, *note*.

Isaiah, his reproof to the Jews for the inconsistency of their outward humiliations with their *oppressive* conduct to the poor, 19. His denunciation against the city of Tyre, 237, *note*.

Judah,

Judah, remarkable deliverance of, from the bondage of Pekah king of Israel, by four chiefs of the children of Ephraim, 322.

L.

Liberty, the deprivation of, the greatest of all injuries, except the loss of life, 301.

Lives, a general view of the melancholy destruction of, in the prosecution of the slave trade, 148, *note*.

Lowth, Dr. examination of his opinion concerning the successor of Josiah king of Judah, as mentioned by the prophet Jeremiah, 52, *note*. His interpretation of the word *pastor*, 162, *note*.

M.

Masquerades, the baneful tendency of, 146, *note*.

Micah, his denunciation of God's vengeance against the Ammonites for their covetous violence, 241, *note*.

N.

Nations, not like individuals, to be called to a future account for their crimes, but receive their punishments in their collective capacity in this world, 253, *note*. Are, by divine wisdom, made mutual scourges to each other, 256.

National wickedness, has generally been visited by *national* punishments, 10, 253, *note*, 259, *note*.

Nebuchadnezzar king of Babylon, the nations commanded to submit to his yoke, 63, *note*, 66. Kills Jehoiakim, 99. His extensive conquests, 124. Executes the decree of God against king Zedekiah, 202. His conduct considered, 207.

Slavery and oppression, the *public* toleration of, a moſt heinous *national* crime in the ſight of God, 10. Strong prophetical deſcription of, 154 Warning hints for the ſtopping of, communicated by the Author to the Britiſh Miniſtry, 251, 252, *notes*.

Soldiers, African, their deplorable ſituation in the company's ſettlements, 150, *note*.

Syrians, the denunciations of the prophet Amos againſt them for their oppreſſions, how fulfilled, 230.

T.

Tyrants, tremendous examples of God's vengeance againſt, to be found in all hiſtories, particularly that of the Jews, 11.

Tyre and Zidon, the ports for the ancient ſlave trade, of Paleſtine, 219. How this wicked traffic was retaliated upon them, 222, *note*. The government of Tyre ſubverted by the ſlaves, 256, *note*.

V.

Vices, deſtructive of national proſperity, 165, *note*. Public, how puniſhed, 253, *note*.

Virginia, petition of the houſe of burgeſſes to the king on the inhumanity and dangerous tendency of the African *ſlave-trade*, 306.

Urijah the prophet murdered by Jehoiakim king of Judah, 77.

Uſher, Abp. his account of Nabuchadonoſor king of Babylon, 55, *note*. His opinion as to the king addreſſed by the prophet Jeremiah, ch. xxii. corrected, 136, *note*.

W. War,

W.

War, barbarity in, will incur the vengeance of God, 240, *note*.

X.

Xenophon, his account of the destruction of Babylon, 287, 288, 295.

Y.

Yokes, prophetically used as emblems of *slavery*, 52, *note*, 56, 64.

Z.

Zedekiah king of Judah, prophetic denunciations against him for injustice and oppression, 26. Exhortations to him, 37. Historical account of that prince, 44, 59. Is raised to the throne by Nebuchadnezzar, 108. Exposition of his regal name, 110, 166. Rebels against the king of Babylon, 119. The prophet Jeremiah's message to him particularly considered, 131. Proclaims *liberty* to bondsmen, 172. Denunciations upon his relapse, 177. Judgement executed on him, by the hand of his conqueror Nebuchadnezzar, 202.

☞ This Tract having been unavoidably extended to a much greater length than was at first intended, the Extract from Mr. Morgan's Book, mentioned in p. 258, is inserted in the Appendix of another Tract, intituled, " *The just Limitation of Slavery* " *in the Laws of God compared with the unbound-* " *ed Claims of the African Traders and British* " *American Slave-holders.*"

F I N I S.

Tracts by the same AUTHOR.

Printed for B. WHITE, at HORACE'S-HEAD, FLEET-STREET.

I. A Short Treatise on the English Tongue. Being an Attempt to render the Reading and Pronunciation of the same more easy to Foreigners. 1767.

II. Remarks on several very important Prophecies, first Edition, in 1768, (second Edition, 1775.)

This Book contains, 1st, Remarks on the Prophecy of Isaiah vii. 13–16.—That *a Virgin should conceive and bear a Son*. 2dly, Remarks on the Nature and Style of prophetical Writings. 3dly, Remarks on the Accomplishment of Isaiah's Prophecy, (vii. 8.) " *Within threescore and five Years shall Ephraim be broken, that it* " *be not a People.*" 4thly, On the Departure of the *Sceptre* and *Lawgiver* from Judah. 5thly, A Confirmation of the above Remarks by farther Examples drawn from the Prophets, &c.

III. A Representation of the Injustice and dangerous Tendency of *Tolerating Slavery*; or of admitting the least Claim of *Private Property in the Persons of Men* IN ENGLAND. Being an Answer to an Opinion, given in the Year 1729, by the (then) Attorney General and Solicitor General, concerning the Case of *Slaves* in GREAT-BRITAIN. 1769.

This Tract contains many Examples of the monstrous *Iniquity* and *Injustice* of the Plantation Laws respecting Slaves; as also some Account of the gradual Abolition of the ancient English *Slavery* called VILLENAGE, which was at length happily effected by the Wisdom and Perseverance of the English Courts of Common Law.

IV. Remarks concerning the Encroachments on the River Thames near *Durham-Yard*. 1771.

V.

V. An Appendix to the Reprefentation of the Injuftice and dangerous Tendency of tolerating Slavery. (See Number III.) 1772.

VI. Remarks on the Opinions of fome of the moft celebrated Writers on CROWN LAW, refpecting the due Diftinction between *Manflaughter* and *Murder*; fhewing that the Indulgence allowed by the Courts to *voluntary Manflaughter* in Rencounters, DUELS, &c. is *indifcriminate* and without Foundation in Law; and is alfo one of the principal Caufes of the Continuance and prefent Increafe of the *bafe* and *difgraceful* Practice of DUELLING. 1773.

The peculiar Cafe of *Gentlemen in the Army*, refpecting the Practice of DUELLING, is carefully examined in this Tract; as alfo the Depravity and Folly of *modern Men of Honour* falfely fo called.

VII. In two Parts. 1. A Declaration of the People's *Natural Right* to a Share in the Legiflature; which is the fundamental Principle of *the Britifh Conftitution of State*. 2. A Declaration, or Defence, of the *the fame Doctrine*, when applied *particularly to* THE PEOPLE OF IRELAND. 1774. (2d Edition, 1775.)

In thefe two Pieces many Examples and Proofs are produced concerning *the parliamentary Rights of the People*; viz. That the Affent of the People is abfolutely neceffary to render Laws *valid*: That a *free* and *equal* Reprefentation of the Inhabitants of this Kingdom is neceffary for the *Salvation* of the State, and the Security of *Peace* and of *Property*: That the Reprefentatives of the People have no *legal* Right to give affent in any " *new Device without Conference with* " *their Countries*:" That it is an ancient and juft Right of the People to elect a *new* Parliament " *every Year once, and more often* " *if Need be*;" and that no Regulations whatfoever, wherein the Reprefentatives are made *Judges of their own Elections*, can be effectual againft national Corruption! Examples are likewife here given of feveral *furreptitious* STATUTES that are void through the Want of *due legal Affent*; and of Others that are *void* by being
unjuft

unjust and repugnant to *constitutional Principles!* The Danger of keeping *standing Armies* is also demonstrated, and the Wickedness and Impolicy of Acting by *national Corruption!* &c. &c.

The following Tracts by the same AUTHOR

ARE

Printed for B. WHITE, in FLEET-STREET, and E. and C. DILLY, in the POULTRY.

VIII. The just Limitation of *Slavery* in the *Laws of God*, compared with the unbounded Claims of *the African Traders* and *British American Slave-holders.*

To this Piece is added a copious Appendix, containing, An Answer to the Rev. Mr. *Thompson's* Tract in Favour of the *African Slave-Trade.* Letters concerning *the lineal Descent of the Negroes* from the Sons of HAM. The *Spanish* Regulations for the gradual Enfranchisement of Slaves. A Proposal, on the same Principles, for the gradual Enfranchisement of Slaves in *America.* REPORTS of Determinations in the several COURTS OF LAW against Slavery, &c. 1776.

IX. THE LAW *of* PASSIVE OBEDIENCE; or Christian Submission to personal Injuries:

Wherein is shewn that the several Texts of Scripture, which command the entire Submission of *Servants* or *Slaves* to their *Masters*, cannot authorize the *latter to exact an involuntary Servitude*, nor in the least Degree justify the Claims of modern *Slave-holders*; and also that the several Texts, which enjoin *Submission* to *Rulers, Magistrates,* &c. do not in any Respect authorize the dangerous Doctrine of *an unlimited passive Obedience.*

X. " THE LAW OF LIBERTY ;" or (as it is called in Scripture *by way of Eminence*) " the *Royal Law,*" by which *all Mankind* will certainly *be judged!*

XI.

XI. THE LAW OF RETRIBUTION; or a serious Warning to *Great-Britain* and her *Colonies*, founded on unquestionable Examples of GOD's temporal Vengeance against Tyrants, Slave-holders, and Oppressors. 1776.

The Examples are selected from Predictions, in the Old-Testament, of *national* Judgements, which (being compared with the actual Accomplishment) demonstrate " the sure Word of Prophecy," as well as the immediate Interposition of divine Providence, to recompence impenitent *Nations* according to their Works.

Tracts, by the same AUTHOR, *now in the Press for Publication.*

XII. A Tract *on the Law of Nature* and Principles of Action in Man.

XIII. THE CASE OF SAUL; being an Appendage to the former Tract, wherein the *compound Nature* and various *Principles of Action in* MAN (with the Reality of *supernatural spiritual Influence,* both *good* and *bad)* are proved by unquestionable Examples from the History of that unfortunate Monarch, and also from many other Parts of Scripture.

www.ingramcontent.com/pod-product-compliance
Lightning Source LLC
Chambersburg PA
CBHW021844230426
43669CB00008B/1078